Mometrix

TEST PREPARATION

Secrets of the

CPIM®

Execution and Control of Operations Exam Study Guide

DEAR FUTURE EXAM SUCCESS STORY

First of all, **THANK YOU** for purchasing Mometrix study materials!

Second, congratulations! You are one of the few determined test-takers who are committed to doing whatever it takes to excel on your exam. **You have come to the right place.** We developed these study materials with one goal in mind: to deliver you the information you need in a format that's concise and easy to use.

In addition to optimizing your guide for the content of the test, we've outlined our recommended steps for breaking down the preparation process into small, attainable goals so you can make sure you stay on track.

We've also analyzed the entire test-taking process, identifying the most common pitfalls and showing how you can overcome them and be ready for any curveball the test throws you.

Standardized testing is one of the biggest obstacles on your road to success, which only increases the importance of doing well in the high-pressure, high-stakes environment of test day. Your results on this test could have a significant impact on your future, and this guide provides the information and practical advice to help you achieve your full potential on test day.

Your success is our success

We would love to hear from you! If you would like to share the story of your exam success or if you have any questions or comments in regard to our products, please contact us at **800-673-8175** or **support@mometrix.com**.

Thanks again for your business and we wish you continued success!

Sincerely,
The Mometrix Test Preparation Team

Need more help? Check out our flashcards at:
http://mometrixflashcards.com/CPIM

Written and edited by the Mometrix Exam Secrets Test Prep Team
Printed in the United States of America

Table of Contents

Introduction 1
Secret Key #1 – Plan Big, Study Small 2
Secret Key #2 – Make Your Studying Count 3
Secret Key #3 – Practice the Right Way 4
Secret Key #4 – Pace Yourself 6
Secret Key #5 – Have a Plan for Guessing 7
Test-Taking Strategies 10
Prioritizing and Sequencing Work to be Performed 15
Executing Plans, Implementing Physical Controls, and Reporting Results of Activities Performed 62
Evaluating Performance and Providing Feedback 91
CPIM Practice Test 111
Answer Key and Explanations 120
How to Overcome Test Anxiety 128
Online Resources 134

Introduction

Thank you for purchasing this resource! You have made the choice to prepare yourself for a test that could have a huge impact on your future, and this guide is designed to help you be fully ready for test day. Obviously, it's important to have a solid understanding of the test material, but you also need to be prepared for the unique environment and stressors of the test, so that you can perform to the best of your abilities.

For this purpose, the first section that appears in this guide is the **Secret Keys**. We've devoted countless hours to meticulously researching what works and what doesn't, and we've boiled down our findings to the five most impactful steps you can take to improve your performance on the test. We start at the beginning with study planning and move through the preparation process, all the way to the testing strategies that will help you get the most out of what you know when you're finally sitting in front of the test.

We recommend that you start preparing for your test as far in advance as possible. However, if you've bought this guide as a last-minute study resource and only have a few days before your test, we recommend that you skip over the first two Secret Keys since they address a long-term study plan.

If you struggle with **test anxiety**, we strongly encourage you to check out our recommendations for how you can overcome it. Test anxiety is a formidable foe, but it can be beaten, and we want to make sure you have the tools you need to defeat it.

Secret Key #1 – Plan Big, Study Small

There's a lot riding on your performance. If you want to ace this test, you're going to need to keep your skills sharp and the material fresh in your mind. You need a plan that lets you review everything you need to know while still fitting in your schedule. We'll break this strategy down into three categories.

Information Organization

Start with the information you already have: the official test outline. From this, you can make a complete list of all the concepts you need to cover before the test. Organize these concepts into groups that can be studied together, and create a list of any related vocabulary you need to learn so you can brush up on any difficult terms. You'll want to keep this vocabulary list handy once you actually start studying since you may need to add to it along the way.

Time Management

Once you have your set of study concepts, decide how to spread them out over the time you have left before the test. Break your study plan into small, clear goals so you have a manageable task for each day and know exactly what you're doing. Then just focus on one small step at a time. When you manage your time this way, you don't need to spend hours at a time studying. Studying a small block of content for a short period each day helps you retain information better and avoid stressing over how much you have left to do. You can relax knowing that you have a plan to cover everything in time. In order for this strategy to be effective though, you have to start studying early and stick to your schedule. Avoid the exhaustion and futility that comes from last-minute cramming!

Study Environment

The environment you study in has a big impact on your learning. Studying in a coffee shop, while probably more enjoyable, is not likely to be as fruitful as studying in a quiet room. It's important to keep distractions to a minimum. You're only planning to study for a short block of time, so make the most of it. Don't pause to check your phone or get up to find a snack. It's also important to **avoid multitasking**. Research has consistently shown that multitasking will make your studying dramatically less effective. Your study area should also be comfortable and well-lit so you don't have the distraction of straining your eyes or sitting on an uncomfortable chair.

The time of day you study is also important. You want to be rested and alert. Don't wait until just before bedtime. Study when you'll be most likely to comprehend and remember. Even better, if you know what time of day your test will be, set that time aside for study. That way your brain will be used to working on that subject at that specific time and you'll have a better chance of recalling information.

Finally, it can be helpful to team up with others who are studying for the same test. Your actual studying should be done in as isolated an environment as possible, but the work of organizing the information and setting up the study plan can be divided up. In between study sessions, you can discuss with your teammates the concepts that you're all studying and quiz each other on the details. Just be sure that your teammates are as serious about the test as you are. If you find that your study time is being replaced with social time, you might need to find a new team.

Secret Key #2 – Make Your Studying Count

You're devoting a lot of time and effort to preparing for this test, so you want to be absolutely certain it will pay off. This means doing more than just reading the content and hoping you can remember it on test day. It's important to make every minute of study count. There are two main areas you can focus on to make your studying count.

Retention

It doesn't matter how much time you study if you can't remember the material. You need to make sure you are retaining the concepts. To check your retention of the information you're learning, try recalling it at later times with minimal prompting. Try carrying around flashcards and glance at one or two from time to time or ask a friend who's also studying for the test to quiz you.

To enhance your retention, look for ways to put the information into practice so that you can apply it rather than simply recalling it. If you're using the information in practical ways, it will be much easier to remember. Similarly, it helps to solidify a concept in your mind if you're not only reading it to yourself but also explaining it to someone else. Ask a friend to let you teach them about a concept you're a little shaky on (or speak aloud to an imaginary audience if necessary). As you try to summarize, define, give examples, and answer your friend's questions, you'll understand the concepts better and they will stay with you longer. Finally, step back for a big picture view and ask yourself how each piece of information fits with the whole subject. When you link the different concepts together and see them working together as a whole, it's easier to remember the individual components.

Finally, practice showing your work on any multi-step problems, even if you're just studying. Writing out each step you take to solve a problem will help solidify the process in your mind, and you'll be more likely to remember it during the test.

Modality

Modality simply refers to the means or method by which you study. Choosing a study modality that fits your own individual learning style is crucial. No two people learn best in exactly the same way, so it's important to know your strengths and use them to your advantage.

For example, if you learn best by visualization, focus on visualizing a concept in your mind and draw an image or a diagram. Try color-coding your notes, illustrating them, or creating symbols that will trigger your mind to recall a learned concept. If you learn best by hearing or discussing information, find a study partner who learns the same way or read aloud to yourself. Think about how to put the information in your own words. Imagine that you are giving a lecture on the topic and record yourself so you can listen to it later.

For any learning style, flashcards can be helpful. Organize the information so you can take advantage of spare moments to review. Underline key words or phrases. Use different colors for different categories. Mnemonic devices (such as creating a short list in which every item starts with the same letter) can also help with retention. Find what works best for you and use it to store the information in your mind most effectively and easily.

Secret Key #3 – Practice the Right Way

Your success on test day depends not only on how many hours you put into preparing, but also on whether you prepared the right way. It's good to check along the way to see if your studying is paying off. One of the most effective ways to do this is by taking practice tests to evaluate your progress. Practice tests are useful because they show exactly where you need to improve. Every time you take a practice test, pay special attention to these three groups of questions:

- The questions you got wrong
- The questions you had to guess on, even if you guessed right
- The questions you found difficult or slow to work through

This will show you exactly what your weak areas are, and where you need to devote more study time. Ask yourself why each of these questions gave you trouble. Was it because you didn't understand the material? Was it because you didn't remember the vocabulary? Do you need more repetitions on this type of question to build speed and confidence? Dig into those questions and figure out how you can strengthen your weak areas as you go back to review the material.

Additionally, many practice tests have a section explaining the answer choices. It can be tempting to read the explanation and think that you now have a good understanding of the concept. However, an explanation likely only covers part of the question's broader context. Even if the explanation makes perfect sense, **go back and investigate** every concept related to the question until you're positive you have a thorough understanding.

As you go along, keep in mind that the practice test is just that: practice. Memorizing these questions and answers will not be very helpful on the actual test because it is unlikely to have any of the same exact questions. If you only know the right answers to the sample questions, you won't be prepared for the real thing. **Study the concepts** until you understand them fully, and then you'll be able to answer any question that shows up on the test.

It's important to wait on the practice tests until you're ready. If you take a test on your first day of study, you may be overwhelmed by the amount of material covered and how much you need to learn. Work up to it gradually.

On test day, you'll need to be prepared for answering questions, managing your time, and using the test-taking strategies you've learned. It's a lot to balance, like a mental marathon that will have a big impact on your future. Like training for a marathon, you'll need to start slowly and work your way up. When test day arrives, you'll be ready.

Start with the strategies you've read in the first two Secret Keys—plan your course and study in the way that works best for you. If you have time, consider using multiple study resources to get different approaches to the same concepts. It can be helpful to see difficult concepts from more than one angle. Then find a good source for practice tests. Many times, the test website will suggest potential study resources or provide sample tests.

Practice Test Strategy

If you're able to find at least three practice tests, we recommend this strategy:

Untimed and Open-Book Practice

Take the first test with no time constraints and with your notes and study guide handy. Take your time and focus on applying the strategies you've learned.

Timed and Open-Book Practice

Take the second practice test open-book as well, but set a timer and practice pacing yourself to finish in time.

Timed and Closed-Book Practice

Take any other practice tests as if it were test day. Set a timer and put away your study materials. Sit at a table or desk in a quiet room, imagine yourself at the testing center, and answer questions as quickly and accurately as possible.

Keep repeating timed and closed-book tests on a regular basis until you run out of practice tests or it's time for the actual test. Your mind will be ready for the schedule and stress of test day, and you'll be able to focus on recalling the material you've learned.

Secret Key #4 – Pace Yourself

Once you're fully prepared for the material on the test, your biggest challenge on test day will be managing your time. Just knowing that the clock is ticking can make you panic even if you have plenty of time left. Work on pacing yourself so you can build confidence against the time constraints of the exam. Pacing is a difficult skill to master, especially in a high-pressure environment, so **practice is vital**.

Set time expectations for your pace based on how much time is available. For example, if a section has 60 questions and the time limit is 30 minutes, you know you have to average 30 seconds or less per question in order to answer them all. Although 30 seconds is the hard limit, set 25 seconds per question as your goal, so you reserve extra time to spend on harder questions. When you budget extra time for the harder questions, you no longer have any reason to stress when those questions take longer to answer.

Don't let this time expectation distract you from working through the test at a calm, steady pace, but keep it in mind so you don't spend too much time on any one question. Recognize that taking extra time on one question you don't understand may keep you from answering two that you do understand later in the test. If your time limit for a question is up and you're still not sure of the answer, mark it and move on, and come back to it later if the time and the test format allow. If the testing format doesn't allow you to return to earlier questions, just make an educated guess; then put it out of your mind and move on.

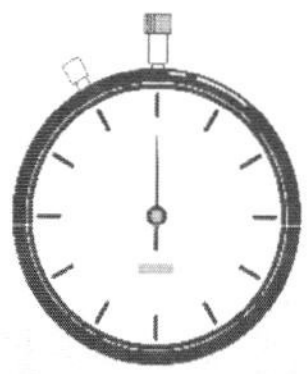

On the easier questions, be careful not to rush. It may seem wise to hurry through them so you have more time for the challenging ones, but it's not worth missing one if you know the concept and just didn't take the time to read the question fully. Work efficiently but make sure you understand the question and have looked at all of the answer choices, since more than one may seem right at first.

Even if you're paying attention to the time, you may find yourself a little behind at some point. You should speed up to get back on track, but do so wisely. Don't panic; just take a few seconds less on each question until you're caught up. Don't guess without thinking, but do look through the answer choices and eliminate any you know are wrong. If you can get down to two choices, it is often worthwhile to guess from those. Once you've chosen an answer, move on and don't dwell on any that you skipped or had to hurry through. If a question was taking too long, chances are it was one of the harder ones, so you weren't as likely to get it right anyway.

On the other hand, if you find yourself getting ahead of schedule, it may be beneficial to slow down a little. The more quickly you work, the more likely you are to make a careless mistake that will affect your score. You've budgeted time for each question, so don't be afraid to spend that time. Practice an efficient but careful pace to get the most out of the time you have.

Secret Key #5 – Have a Plan for Guessing

When you're taking the test, you may find yourself stuck on a question. Some of the answer choices seem better than others, but you don't see the one answer choice that is obviously correct. What do you do?

The scenario described above is very common, yet most test takers have not effectively prepared for it. Developing and practicing a plan for guessing may be one of the single most effective uses of your time as you get ready for the exam.

In developing your plan for guessing, there are three questions to address:

- When should you start the guessing process?
- How should you narrow down the choices?
- Which answer should you choose?

When to Start the Guessing Process

Unless your plan for guessing is to select C every time (which, despite its merits, is not what we recommend), you need to leave yourself enough time to apply your answer elimination strategies. Since you have a limited amount of time for each question, that means that if you're going to give yourself the best shot at guessing correctly, you have to decide quickly whether or not you will guess.

Of course, the best-case scenario is that you don't have to guess at all, so first, see if you can answer the question based on your knowledge of the subject and basic reasoning skills. Focus on the key words in the question and try to jog your memory of related topics. Give yourself a chance to bring the knowledge to mind, but once you realize that you don't have (or you can't access) the knowledge you need to answer the question, it's time to start the guessing process.

It's almost always better to start the guessing process too early than too late. It only takes a few seconds to remember something and answer the question from knowledge. Carefully eliminating wrong answer choices takes longer. Plus, going through the process of eliminating answer choices can actually help jog your memory.

Summary: Start the guessing process as soon as you decide that you can't answer the question based on your knowledge.

How to Narrow Down the Choices

The next chapter in this book (**Test-Taking Strategies**) includes a wide range of strategies for how to approach questions and how to look for answer choices to eliminate. You will definitely want to read those carefully, practice them, and figure out which ones work best for you. Here though, we're going to address a mindset rather than a particular strategy.

Your odds of guessing an answer correctly depend on how many options you are choosing from.

Number of options left	5	4	3	2	1
Odds of guessing correctly	20%	25%	33%	50%	100%

You can see from this chart just how valuable it is to be able to eliminate incorrect answers and make an educated guess, but there are two things that many test takers do that cause them to miss out on the benefits of guessing:

- Accidentally eliminating the correct answer
- Selecting an answer based on an impression

We'll look at the first one here, and the second one in the next section.

To avoid accidentally eliminating the correct answer, we recommend a thought exercise called **the $5 challenge**. In this challenge, you only eliminate an answer choice from contention if you are willing to bet $5 on it being wrong. Why $5? Five dollars is a small but not insignificant amount of money. It's an amount you could afford to lose but wouldn't want to throw away. And while losing $5 once might not hurt too much, doing it twenty times will set you back $100. In the same way, each small decision you make—eliminating a choice here, guessing on a question there—won't by itself impact your score very much, but when you put them all together, they can make a big difference. By holding each answer choice elimination decision to a higher standard, you can reduce the risk of accidentally eliminating the correct answer.

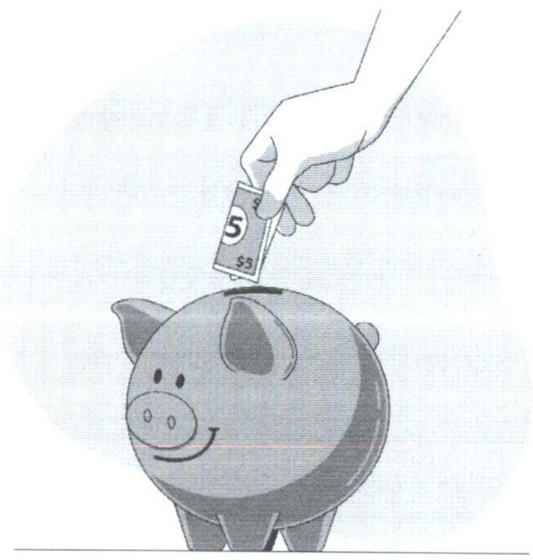

The $5 challenge can also be applied in a positive sense: If you are willing to bet $5 that an answer choice *is* correct, go ahead and mark it as correct.

Summary: Only eliminate an answer choice if you are willing to bet $5 that it is wrong.

Which Answer to Choose

You're taking the test. You've run into a hard question and decided you'll have to guess. You've eliminated all the answer choices you're willing to bet $5 on. Now you have to pick an answer. Why do we even need to talk about this? Why can't you just pick whichever one you feel like when the time comes?

The answer to these questions is that if you don't come into the test with a plan, you'll rely on your impression to select an answer choice, and if you do that, you risk falling into a trap. The test writers know that everyone who takes their test will be guessing on some of the questions, so they intentionally write wrong answer choices to seem plausible. You still have to pick an answer though, and if the wrong answer choices are designed to look right, how can you ever be sure that you're not falling for their trap? The best solution we've found to this dilemma is to take the decision out of your hands entirely. Here is the process we recommend:

Once you've eliminated any choices that you are confident (willing to bet $5) are wrong, select the first remaining choice as your answer.

Whether you choose to select the first remaining choice, the second, or the last, the important thing is that you use some preselected standard. Using this approach guarantees that you will not be enticed into selecting an answer choice that looks right, because you are not basing your decision on how the answer choices look.

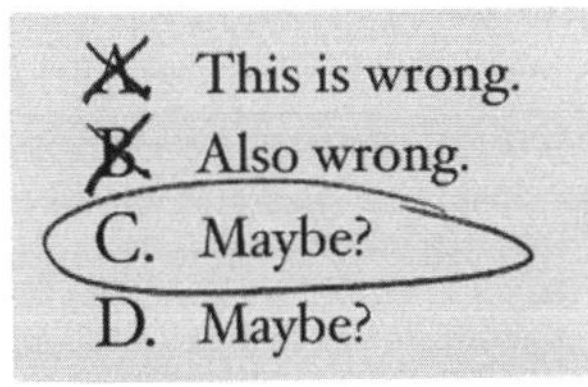

This is not meant to make you question your knowledge. Instead, it is to help you recognize the difference between your knowledge and your impressions. There's a huge difference between thinking an answer is right because of what you know, and thinking an answer is right because it looks or sounds like it should be right.

Summary: To ensure that your selection is appropriately random, make a predetermined selection from among all answer choices you have not eliminated.

Test-Taking Strategies

This section contains a list of test-taking strategies that you may find helpful as you work through the test. By taking what you know and applying logical thought, you can maximize your chances of answering any question correctly!

It is very important to realize that every question is different and every person is different: no single strategy will work on every question, and no single strategy will work for every person. That's why we've included all of them here, so you can try them out and determine which ones work best for different types of questions and which ones work best for you.

Question Strategies

✓ Read Carefully

Read the question and the answer choices carefully. Don't miss the question because you misread the terms. You have plenty of time to read each question thoroughly and make sure you understand what is being asked. Yet a happy medium must be attained, so don't waste too much time. You must read carefully and efficiently.

✓ Contextual Clues

Look for contextual clues. If the question includes a word you are not familiar with, look at the immediate context for some indication of what the word might mean. Contextual clues can often give you all the information you need to decipher the meaning of an unfamiliar word. Even if you can't determine the meaning, you may be able to narrow down the possibilities enough to make a solid guess at the answer to the question.

✓ Prefixes

If you're having trouble with a word in the question or answer choices, try dissecting it. Take advantage of every clue that the word might include. Prefixes can be a huge help. Usually, they allow you to determine a basic meaning. *Pre-* means before, *post-* means after, *pro-* is positive, *de-* is negative. From prefixes, you can get an idea of the general meaning of the word and try to put it into context.

✓ Hedge Words

Watch out for critical hedge words, such as *likely, may, can, often, almost, mostly, usually, generally, rarely,* and *sometimes.* Question writers insert these hedge phrases to cover every possibility. Often an answer choice will be wrong simply because it leaves no room for exception. Be on guard for answer choices that have definitive words such as *exactly* and *always.*

✓ Switchback Words

Stay alert for *switchbacks.* These are the words and phrases frequently used to alert you to shifts in thought. The most common switchback words are *but, although,* and *however.* Others include *nevertheless, on the other hand, even though, while, in spite of, despite,* and *regardless of.* Switchback words are important to catch because they can change the direction of the question or an answer choice.

☑ Face Value

When in doubt, use common sense. Accept the situation in the problem at face value. Don't read too much into it. These problems will not require you to make wild assumptions. If you have to go beyond creativity and warp time or space in order to have an answer choice fit the question, then you should move on and consider the other answer choices. These are normal problems rooted in reality. The applicable relationship or explanation may not be readily apparent, but it is there for you to figure out. Use your common sense to interpret anything that isn't clear.

Answer Choice Strategies

☑ Answer Selection

The most thorough way to pick an answer choice is to identify and eliminate wrong answers until only one is left, then confirm it is the correct answer. Sometimes an answer choice may immediately seem right, but be careful. The test writers will usually put more than one reasonable answer choice on each question, so take a second to read all of them and make sure that the other choices are not equally obvious. As long as you have time left, it is better to read every answer choice than to pick the first one that looks right without checking the others.

☑ Answer Choice Families

An answer choice family consists of two (in rare cases, three) answer choices that are very similar in construction and cannot all be true at the same time. If you see two answer choices that are direct opposites or parallels, one of them is usually the correct answer. For instance, if one answer choice says that quantity *x* increases and another either says that quantity *x* decreases (opposite) or says that quantity *y* increases (parallel), then those answer choices would fall into the same family. An answer choice that doesn't match the construction of the answer choice family is more likely to be incorrect. Most questions will not have answer choice families, but when they do appear, you should be prepared to recognize them.

☑ Eliminate Answers

Eliminate answer choices as soon as you realize they are wrong, but make sure you consider all possibilities. If you are eliminating answer choices and realize that the last one you are left with is also wrong, don't panic. Start over and consider each choice again. There may be something you missed the first time that you will realize on the second pass.

☑ Avoid Fact Traps

Don't be distracted by an answer choice that is factually true but doesn't answer the question. You are looking for the choice that answers the question. Stay focused on what the question is asking for so you don't accidentally pick an answer that is true but incorrect. Always go back to the question and make sure the answer choice you've selected actually answers the question and is not merely a true statement.

☑ Extreme Statements

In general, you should avoid answers that put forth extreme actions as standard practice or proclaim controversial ideas as established fact. An answer choice that states the "process should be used in certain situations, if..." is much more likely to be correct than one that states the "process should be discontinued completely." The first is a calm rational statement and doesn't even make a definitive, uncompromising stance, using a hedge word *if* to provide wiggle room, whereas the second choice is far more extreme.

⊘ BENCHMARK

As you read through the answer choices and you come across one that seems to answer the question well, mentally select that answer choice. This is not your final answer, but it's the one that will help you evaluate the other answer choices. The one that you selected is your benchmark or standard for judging each of the other answer choices. Every other answer choice must be compared to your benchmark. That choice is correct until proven otherwise by another answer choice beating it. If you find a better answer, then that one becomes your new benchmark. Once you've decided that no other choice answers the question as well as your benchmark, you have your final answer.

⊘ PREDICT THE ANSWER

Before you even start looking at the answer choices, it is often best to try to predict the answer. When you come up with the answer on your own, it is easier to avoid distractions and traps because you will know exactly what to look for. The right answer choice is unlikely to be word-for-word what you came up with, but it should be a close match. Even if you are confident that you have the right answer, you should still take the time to read each option before moving on.

General Strategies

⊘ TOUGH QUESTIONS

If you are stumped on a problem or it appears too hard or too difficult, don't waste time. Move on! Remember though, if you can quickly check for obviously incorrect answer choices, your chances of guessing correctly are greatly improved. Before you completely give up, at least try to knock out a couple of possible answers. Eliminate what you can and then guess at the remaining answer choices before moving on.

⊘ CHECK YOUR WORK

Since you will probably not know every term listed and the answer to every question, it is important that you get credit for the ones that you do know. Don't miss any questions through careless mistakes. If at all possible, try to take a second to look back over your answer selection and make sure you've selected the correct answer choice and haven't made a costly careless mistake (such as marking an answer choice that you didn't mean to mark). This quick double check should more than pay for itself in caught mistakes for the time it costs.

⊘ PACE YOURSELF

It's easy to be overwhelmed when you're looking at a page full of questions; your mind is confused and full of random thoughts, and the clock is ticking down faster than you would like. Calm down and maintain the pace that you have set for yourself. Especially as you get down to the last few minutes of the test, don't let the small numbers on the clock make you panic. As long as you are on track by monitoring your pace, you are guaranteed to have time for each question.

⊘ DON'T RUSH

It is very easy to make errors when you are in a hurry. Maintaining a fast pace in answering questions is pointless if it makes you miss questions that you would have gotten right otherwise. Test writers like to include distracting information and wrong answers that seem right. Taking a little extra time to avoid careless mistakes can make all the difference in your test score. Find a pace that allows you to be confident in the answers that you select.

⊘ Keep Moving

Panicking will not help you pass the test, so do your best to stay calm and keep moving. Taking deep breaths and going through the answer elimination steps you practiced can help to break through a stress barrier and keep your pace.

Final Notes

The combination of a solid foundation of content knowledge and the confidence that comes from practicing your plan for applying that knowledge is the key to maximizing your performance on test day. As your foundation of content knowledge is built up and strengthened, you'll find that the strategies included in this chapter become more and more effective in helping you quickly sift through the distractions and traps of the test to isolate the correct answer.

Now that you're preparing to move forward into the test content chapters of this book, be sure to keep your goal in mind. As you read, think about how you will be able to apply this information on the test. If you've already seen sample questions for the test and you have an idea of the question format and style, try to come up with questions of your own that you can answer based on what you're reading. This will give you valuable practice applying your knowledge in the same ways you can expect to on test day.

Good luck and good studying!

Prioritizing and Sequencing Work to be Performed

MPC

Manufacturing planning and control (MPC) occurs at three distinct levels or phases.

- Top Management Planning: This includes both sales and operations planning, and resource requirements planning. During this process or phase, top managers set volume requirements by product groups and establish time frames for production.
- Operations Management Planning: OMP, or Operations Management Planning, includes scheduling and material requirement planning, and also sets the parameters for capacity requirements. Capacity testing is done during this phase. The final production plan is detailed by item number and date.
- Operations Management Execution: This refers to the control phase of MPC, during which plans are executed. Components of control are procurement, kanban implementation, and actual production. The procurement component involves negotiating the supply and transportation of materials.

TOP MANAGEMENT PLANNING

Top management planning is the first stage in Management Planning and Control of Manufacturing. One of the tasks which must be addressed by the senior management team is the plan for Sales and Operations.

- Senior management must define the products to be sold.
- Senior management must group manufactured items into family groups.
- Senior management must plan product families far into the future when resources fluctuate and there may not always be enough materials available to meet production schedules and targets.
- Senior management must consider economies of scale as productive capacity comes close to its top levels.

After considering these individual components, the senior top management team must compile its conclusions into separate sales and production plans. The sales plan must be distributed and coordinated with the sales force. The production plan must identify product volumes at specific time periods.

RRP

RRP, or Resource Requirements Planning, is a way of matching resources to production capabilities with a view toward greater efficiency of utilization. APICS describes it as a process of breaking down operational planning into cohesive units and conducting financial planning in terms of dollars. While RRP relies on the use of computers to balance the process, it also relies on human skills and supervision at critical points.

- RRP can anticipate long-term material needs and requirements.
- RRP can analyze and anticipate workloads at critical project points in the manufacturing cycle.

- RRP can balance materials and capacity in a way that prevents shortages or bottlenecks during manufacturing.
- RRP is a testing mechanism that validates the metrics of operational planning and performance.

It is important to recognize that RRP is a combined strategy which involves a variety of planning components and tools. While RRP systems rely on the use of computers, it would be a large mistake to view RRP as simply a software program that does the job of planning and applying resources. At the same time, systems of resource planning are customized plans designed to suit a particular set of circumstances.

- RRP is both an inventory reduction plan and a production control plan.
- RRP involves the general initial planning stage, which is carried out by senior management.
- Subsequent RRP steps involve more detailed planning based on the overall strategy developed by senior management. More detailed planning may involve calculation of manpower and workloads at specific points, production schedules and materials routing, and the establishment of reliable lead times.
- The final steps of RRP involve executing the plan and controlling the process through monitoring and metrics.

RCCP

Rough-Cut Capacity Planning is a phase of manufacturing which is based on Master Production Scheduling.

- RCCP is a method of assessing the feasibility of the Master Planning Schedule.
- RCCP can function as an early warning system of bottlenecked production. RCCP modules provide quantifiable metrics to gauge the size of problems which develop.
- RCCP provides information to management about the workloads at critical points and centers.
- RCCP data can serve as a management tool which allows the production schedulers to revise and adapt schedule planning to meet customer order demands.
- RCCP data can be shared with suppliers and vendors so that critical production and shipping dates can be met.
- RCCP data flows to all work centers involved in materials supply and production. This makes it easier to match productive capacity to the Master Planning Schedule.

CRP

Capacity Requirements Planning compares the standard hours required for manufacturing items to specification with the actual hours available. Comparisons are made for different time periods and dictated by the manufacturing order established by the work center.

- CRP receives order data from MRP and then breaks the orders down into component parts.
- Each part or segment of the manufacturing process is evaluated by multiplying the total number of operations at that work center by standard run time figures.
- The same calculations are made for other work center operations. The total required hours are then matched against the hours available to operate.

The results are usually expressed in table form or through graphic representations. Tables are more specific, but graphic representations of capacity in comparison to available hours are more easily and quickly read and communicated to others.

There are a variety of strategies that should be considered to address the problem of insufficient capacity, which is a common occurrence in real world manufacturing situations. The manager should be aware that a revision of the Master Planning Schedule, although a possible solution, should only be considered as a last resort.

Four basic courses of action may be employed by the manager who needs to increase capacity:

- Overtime is the most frequent method used to increase capacity, and it requires little effort to implement.
- Subcontracting can increase capacity, but requires considerable advance preparation.
- Alternate routing or redistribution of workload can alleviate the problem of insufficient capacity, but can have unforeseen consequences.
- Adding personnel is another way of addressing manpower needs. This works most effectively if the additional workers are drawn from within the ranks and/or from underutilized shifts.

Each of these methods has disadvantages, although they are all effective at increasing capacity.

- Overtime is popular with some workers, but can be costly. Companies work from an annual budget, which often limits the amount of overtime that is possible.
- Subcontracting has a cost disadvantage. If subcontracting could be done at a lower cost than in-house manufacturing, a company would simply buy the finished product from a subcontractor.
- Alternate routing is advantageous so long as re-routing the work produces a high quality product. It is preferable to overtime since it costs less, but it will not be effective if all work stations are overburdened.
- The addition of new personnel presents an additional cost burden. It can be effective if workers can be obtained from an underutilized work center.

If there is enough equipment and the facility is suitable, management may exercise the option to add an additional shift to add new personnel to an overburdened work center. The additional personnel may be new hires, or they may already be employed by the organization. Either way, the addition of personnel can create unique problems:

- Union rules in some states and local areas may restrict this option or prohibit it entirely. Modern unions have shown an increasing flexibility in cross-training since it is beneficial to both workers and the organization for the company to be competitive and for jobs to be secure.
- If the additional personnel are to come from new hires, this must be approved and accounted for in a new budget. Financial departments are impacted. The funds for hiring new personnel cannot be manufactured.
- The addition of new personnel is sometimes prevented by equipment shortages and facility issues. New hiring must be consistent with new purchases of equipment or the expansion of facilities.

MRPII

Manufacturing is an evolutionary process that has been greatly accelerated by the globalization of the marketplace and the technological revolution.

- MRP means Materials Requirements Planning. In its earlier stages, it applied strictly to materials management in planning, purchasing, storing, and transforming through manufacture. MRP was greatly enhanced by the development of management databases and other communications technology.
- MRPII derived from and includes Materials Requirements Planning, but became an expanded form which was integrated into other activities necessary to the process of manufacturing. MRPII capitalized on advances and lower costs in information technology to manage finance and human relations in addition to materials.

MRP II extends the opportunity for better inventory management. Therefore, it is likely that MRP II implementation would benefit from a review of stockroom procedures.

- Managers and other personnel must be educated and trained in the use of MRP II systems and in SPC (statistical process control).
- All personnel stand to benefit from accountability in the transaction processing system of MRP II.
- Assigned error codes should be used to reconcile and correct discrepancies. Documentation errors include missing documents, inventory miscounting, and items in the wrong location.
- Maps of stockroom layout and material flow should be continuously refreshed and prominently displayed.
- Performance output reports must take advantage of SPC capabilities.

Materials Requirements Planning can improve the profit picture by reducing bottlenecks and paring inventory to make it consistent with demand. Traditional MRP has been enhanced by recent developments in technology, which are characteristic of MRP II.

- One of the characteristics of MRP is better coordination between operations managers, materials purchasers, and suppliers, which can drastically reduce inventory carrying costs and storage inventory. Combined MRP II techniques and kanban can form a JIT inventory system, which adds profitability.
- Improvements in throughput reduction of factory lead times leads to advantages on the liability side of the balance sheet because it speeds up the cash conversion cycle. Improvements in the cash conversion cycle means less debt service for the company.
- The CCC, or cash conversion cycle, represents the time it takes for a company to receive an order, manufacture it, deliver a product, and receive cash payment. Short cash conversion cycles are associated with the efficient use of the plant, equipment, and warehouses.

MPS, PFCS, AND MES

Manufacturing systems, policies, and philosophies are in a constant state of flux as new communications technologies add speed to manufacturing processes.

MES, or Manufacturing Execution System, software is a process that developed in the gap between Master Product Scheduling and Plant Floor Control Systems (PFCS). MES is an integration of both methodologies that supports accurate data sharing between components.

- Whereas MPS monitored production in terms of days, weeks, and months, the factory floor (PFCS) monitored machines and equipment in real time: seconds, nanoseconds, etc.
- MPS data is focused on financial information, routing, BOM, and other data. PFCS employs programmable logic controllers (PLCs).
- MPS relies heavily on data supplied through manual input or bar code scanners. PFCS is more immediate, and may obtain data from intelligent devices like RFID readers.

MPS is focused on the entire plant, whereas PFCS generates data from each machine or from groups of machines.

Manufacturing Environments

APICS definitions of the four basic manufacturing environments are based on quantities and varieties of manufactured products. The choices factory planners have to make are based on the range of quantities and the range of varieties. It would not make sense to design a low-volume factory output scheme around a product that is used in high quantities. A company that manufactures a wide variety of nails, for example, must be designed around high volumes and a wide variety of sizes.

The four basic manufacturing environments defined by APICS are the job shop environment, batch manufacturing, line manufacturing, and continuous manufacturing.

- The job shop is defined by APICS as a facility where like machinery is located and classified by function. For example, a part of the shop is designated the drilling area, while another part of the shop is the sanding area or the painting area.
- Batch manufacturing is a process whereby single orders are processed together as a single lot. A customer may order 2500 pencils, for example, or 4500 T-shirts. These types of facilities are designed to accommodate repeat ordering and production.
- Line manufacturing environments are designed around high volumes and low product variety. The sequence of operations is static, and products on the way to manufacture travel the same path. The manufacture of washing machines is a good example of line manufacturing.

Continuous manufacturing environments produce standard products with very little variance. Toothpaste may be imbued with different colors, tastes, and graphics, but a tube of Crest toothpaste is really not much different than the Crest toothpaste produced two years ago.

Material Planning Requirements

Each of these terms is important to materials planning requirements of efficient manufacturing.

- ATP refers to the quantity of finished product which is "available to promise" and can be delivered to a customer within a specified time period. The finished product is used to fill received orders.
- MPS refers to the Master Production Schedule, an overall plan for the manufacturing endeavor which will eliminate unnecessary processing steps and ensure that manufacturing bottlenecks are not created by such things as capacity limitations or inconsistent materials availability.
- RCCP means "rough-cut capacity planning." This part of the Master Production Schedule determines whether the overall schedule is feasible. At this stage in the process, RCCP is less accurate than when the final Capacity Requirements Planning is complete.

The MS, or Master Schedule, includes many of the planning elements which are absent from the MPS, or Master Production Schedule. One way of thinking about it is that the MPS is the "nuts and bolts" of the Master Scheduling process.

- The MS includes demand forecasts and information about backlogged items for which customer orders have been received. It also encompasses the supply plan, the on-hand inventory, and ATP quantities.
- The MPS may be thought of as the output of the Master Scheduling, or MS, process. The MPS specifies the quantities and groups of final product or completed major component assemblies manufactured at that location.

One of the most significant problems encountered in adapting the Master Production Schedule to the process of Materials Requirement Planning is that the Master Production Schedule does not adequately reflect the facility's operating capacity.

- Planning groups or teams should not assume that sufficient capacity is available to produce materials and components at the exact time they're needed. This capacity insensitivity has led to bottlenecks and inefficient manufacturing.
- An overly optimistic Master Production Schedule orders more production than the manufacturing system can accommodate.
- An overly ambitious MPS causes bottlenecks in raw materials and an increase in pipeline inventories as unfinished final products build up in queues.
- A MPS which is insensitive to production capacity can increase lead times and prevent ordered items from being shipped according to the distribution schedule.

Planning and Control Files

Planning files are used to define a manufacturing operation in detail. Information in the planning files is said to be static because, once defined, the data does not vary as the result of process operation. The three chief types of static files that fall under the category of planning files are the Item Master File, the Routing File, and the Work Center File.

- Item Master File: The master file for an item used in assembly contains extensive information fields describing the specifications and characteristics of the item. It will describe the alloy materials, the size, tolerances, weight, and other characteristics.
- Routing File: This file defines the steps or phases of the assembly process. Each separate operation is defined and the location (work center) where it is to take place is also identified.
- Work Center File: The work center file identifies the work center's capabilities, limitations, and other data which indicates whether an operation is appropriately scheduled to meet demand.

Manufacturers must keep track of WIP, throughput, operations scheduling, and other factors during the process of assembly. This type of information is kept in control files.

- A Shop Order Master File is one type of control file. It consists of a single record for each manufacturing order, and holds information pertaining only to that order. The type of information kept in the Shop Order Master File is data on start date scheduling, completion dates, quantities and volumes, and waste from the production process.
- A Shop Order Detail File is a series of records for each operation. The Shop Order Detail File combines data on planning, scheduling, and priority feeds maintained for the individual work operations.

A key difference between planning files and control files is their level of changeability, or lack of it.

- Information in the planning files is said to be static because, once defined, the data does not vary as the result of process operation.
- Information in control files is dynamic and is constantly updated according to the status of the system operation and the status of manufacturing orders in the system.
- Within the category of planning files are the Item Master File, the Routing File, and the Work Center File.

Within the category of control files are the Shop Order Master File and the Shop Order Detail File.

Manufacturing Plant Layout

Factory plant layout is a vital part of manufacturing planning.

- A poorly configured layout can affect manufacturing efficiency, finished product quality, and costs of manufacturing.
- The physical layout of a plant must be configured properly in the early stages to ensure cost and operations efficiency. It is difficult and expensive to move machines and change traffic and workflow patterns once the design has been set.
- Materials supply areas must be located so as to minimize handling.
- A poor plant configuration will decrease worker efficiencies. A confused flow pattern will cause bottlenecks and result in longer lead times. This may leave managers without flexible alternatives when problems arise.
- The physical configuration and location of machinery determines the pattern in which components and materials will flow through the shop. The right configuration will increase flexibility in manufacturing.

All design planning activities begin with a clear statement of objectives. When designing a manufacturing plant layout, the early considerations are: the volume-variety characteristics of an operation and process types.

Volume-variety characteristics of an operation refer to the types of processes being used for manufacturing. The volume-variety objectives of manufacturing can either be low volume and high variety or high volume and low variety. These properties will determine, to a great extent, the type of design which is best for the manufacturing activity.

A second objective which impacts plant layout is the process type that will be used. Process types may be broken down into categories like:

- Job shop format
- Batch process format
- Continuous flow process
- Mass production process

The basic layout choices for these processes are:

- Process layout
- Cell layout
- Product layout
- Mixed layout

Cell Layouts

A cell layout in a plant facility can enhance the lean manufacturing process. Properly-designed work cells support management efficiency and simplify the flow of materials and the activities of personnel.

The four chief tasks in designing a cell layout are:

- Product selection: The volume-variety concept comes into play and has an impact on the cell layout. Demand forecasting will determine volume-variety requirements. Flow charts should be designed for both high and low volume product flows.
- Process engineering: This includes equipment selection and estimates of set-up times, assembly times, and personnel utilization times.
- Infrastructure design: This should contain flow charts showing external handling of materials and components followed by internal production processes, methods of quality assurance, and other internal handling of completed products.
- Work cell layout: Process charts are a guideline for the physical layout of space and equipment. SPUs (Space Planning Units) are defined.

Cellular Manufacturing

Cellular manufacturing structures may vary significantly. There are work cells in which work flows in a single direction, and there are others where the work flows along a variably circuitous path. No matter what differences exist between the various types of cellular manufacturing structures, there are characteristics which are common to all types of cellular manufacturing. The purpose of a cell is to begin with raw materials or components and end with a finished product.

Machines are of different types, unlike outmoded manufacturing assembly line processes where work moves in batches from areas containing group of machines. The labor force of a cellular manufacturing unit is cross-trained and highly skilled. There is no top-heavy management hierarchy in the cell. Cooperation and control is horizontal, and workers have "ownership" of their products. The work cell produces a single product or a family of similar products.

U-Shaped Cellular Flow Line

The U-shaped cellular flow line is an ideal production process setup for lean operation.

A U-shaped cellular flow line is a U-shaped layout of several different kinds of machines which form a one-piece flow line dedicated to specific tasks.

The U-shape saves floor space and shortens the travel distance between operators at different machines on the line.

The U-shape facilitates communication and visibility between operators working on the products flowing through the line.

U-shaped work cells can be easily configured to accommodate and produce different products within the same family groups. When different products are assigned to U-shaped work cells in this manner, it is termed a multiple-cell flow line.

Synchronous Manufacturing

Synchronous manufacturing refers to the practice of balancing the work in the assembly line so that input is equal to output.

- A proper balance of workloads must be established as the work product moves through a variety of assembly or finishing stations.
- The provision of supplier parts should be stable, whether the supply comes from internal or external supply sources. Supply schedules must be consistent with assembly line demand.
- A kanban system can enhance synchronous manufacturing by delivering the quantities of components or materials needed to balance output.
- Line side bin stocks, floor stocks, and back flushing are practical techniques which enhance synchronized manufacturing.

Focused Manufacturing

Focused manufacturing is said to result from the demands of a target market. Once the products to be manufactured are determined, the facility planners focus the operating methods of the factory so they will be most effective for the targeted products.

- Focused manufacturing produces a limited number of product families with elements in common. The product menu is specific and designed to be efficiently managed at high quality and low cost.
- A focused factory might only produce frying pans or office chairs.
- Focused factories are not geared toward the manufacture of low-volume, high-variety products like customized electronics.
- Giant corporations may have focused manufacturing divisions within their organization, even while other divisions are dedicated to specialized manufacturing processes.

Work Cells

Work cells, groups of work centers arranged into production lines for particular products or product groups, decrease manufacturing lead time by shortening move time and queue time. When the work centers necessary for manufacturing the product are grouped together, work in process is fed directly from one work center to the following adjacent work center. This eliminates moving and queuing except at the initial input into the work cell.

When using JIT, operation set-up times are minimized. Long set-up times increase manufacturing lead time directly and indirectly. The longer the set-up time, the larger the batch size to compensate for the production capacity lost while setting up the manufacturing run. The large batch sizes used when set-up time is long increase the move time and queue time. If set-up time can be cut in half, batch size can be cut in half as well, and the number of manufacturing runs doubled. The same quantity can be produced with significantly reduced queue and wait times due to the smaller batch sizes.

Group Technology and Synchronized Production

Group technology – a factory organizational scheme in which product design and process attributes are analyzed and products are grouped for production in work cells according to similarity in order to standardize processes and set-ups times so goods move through the factory at a faster rate.

Synchronized production – a factory organizational scheme in which all activities at all levels are governed by the overall manufacturing goals; at every level of manufacturing, goods are produced in the quantity and at the time necessary for the next manufacturing level to meet the overall manufacturing goals, so work in progress and semi-finished goods are minimized and not held in storage.

Flow Shop and Job Shop

The flow structure of any manufacturing process impacts the layout of the facility, resources, work methods, and technology decisions.

Production materials and components can take several paths in the job shop, and the activities do not always occur in the same sequence. This type of flexibility is needed to produce customized items in lower volumes. Different products being processed through a job shop will often pass to different work areas. Job shops emphasize the skills of their workers to produce specialized components in a process that is low in efficiency but high in flexibility.

A flow shop is a manufacturing facility in which raw materials or components follow the same path to completion. For example, all materials or components will follow the same sequence, from molding machine, to sanding machine, to painting room, to drying room, to packaging.

Where multiple processes are involved, equipment will be located with a view to reducing material handling and throughput times. Like machines will be positioned so that processing can flow along in a linear fashion. Since all materials and components follow the same path, routing sheets are unnecessary. Flow shop manufacturing is scheduled to fixed run times. Materials and component flow must be balanced by PAC.

A flow shop has a prescribed sequence of steps which are vital to productive manufacturing. For example, all materials or components will follow the same sequence, from molding machine, to sanding machine, to painting room, to drying room, to packaging.

- Quantities of materials and products in a flow shop are typically measured by volume, number, weight, or a combination of all of these.
- Continuous flow shops have little flexibility and higher costs, but they can produce the volumes required by large mass markets.

When multiple processes are involved, equipment in a flow shop will be located with a view to reducing material handling and throughput times.

- Like machines will be positioned so that processing can flow along in a linear fashion.
- Since all materials and components follow the same path, routing sheets are unnecessary.
- Flow shop manufacturing is scheduled to fixed run times.

Materials and component flow must be balanced by PAC.

Flow Control Scheduling

Flow control scheduling is the process of setting production targets or objectives and then controlling the work centers in such a way that those goals are reached.

- Flow control scheduling is most often used in assembly-style manufacturing, wherein a product moves along a set path without variation. Efficiency is achieved through mass production and overlapping workloads.

- Flow control scheduling must be supported by a plant's physical design and layout. Machinery would be positioned in lines rather than having all machines of the same type grouped together. Raw material or component inventory would be conveniently located to cut access times.
- Flow control scheduling requires that run rates be constant so as to meet realistic and efficient production objectives. Workflow and workload balance is determined by schedules rather than manufacturing orders.

Designing a Continuous Flow Line

There is more to creating a continuous flow line than rearranging the furniture in an assembly facility. The steps necessary to create continuous flow involve more than just a layout change.

- Decide which products or product families will go into your cells.
- Determine whether the cells will be product-based or mixed model. Mixed model cells require fast changeover times.
- Calculate Takt Time (a measurement of demand per unit hours)
- Document the steps and phases required for the manufacture of a single unit. Each phase must be timed repeatedly until the most efficient time is obtained.
- Evaluate the capability of equipment to match calculated Takt Time.
- Create a lean layout, which requires less walking and parts handling.
- Balance the cell by determining how many machine operators are required for the cell to meet Takt Time.
- Divide the work within the cell with the objective of meeting Takt Time.

One-Piece Flow Assembly

Traditional batch processing methods result in more handling, more waste, and more inventory buildup, all of which are costly and do not add value to the product.

- Traditional batch processing refers to the sequential manufacture of specific volumes of products until a particular quantity is produced.
- When a batch size or lot has completed the first phase of its manufacturing process, the entire batch is moved to the next sequence in finishing the product.

One piece flow assembly is the process of moving a single item through a flow line to completion.

- One piece flow assembly does not depend on queues or large amounts of inventory.
- One piece flow assembly does not require material handling if work cells are located and designed so that work passes easily from one station to the next.

The Japanese continuous improvement philosophy, known as kaizen, is a principal reason for the high quality products and high productivity associated with that country's manufacturing firms.

- One-piece flow provides an advantage with respect to product quality. With this type of production, every worker is an inspector. Mistakes have a greater chance of being noticed.
- One-piece flow reduces inventory costs since less inventory is required at work stations.
- One-piece flow improves productivity because it allows for multi-process handling, reduced cycle times, and balanced flow lines.
- One-piece flow does not carry a large amount of WIP, as the space between workstations is tight and controlled.

- One-piece flow simplifies replenishment and allows for a variety of replenishment methods, including milk runs, timed deliveries, and programmed quantity deliveries.
- One piece flow improves flexibility and throughput time. The manufacturer can forestall scheduling and still deliver the product on time. It is more responsive.
- One piece flow improves scalability since smaller and less expensive equipment can be designed. Simple processes can be more readily adapted to a relaxed but continuous flow line pace.
- One piece flow does not require the lifting of heavy containers, which results in worker injury and added expenses associated with time lost and worker compensation. One-piece items can be moved without forklifts moving through work areas.
- One piece flow means that every worker on the flow line gets to experience a sense of accomplishment and pride. Morale is improved when workers are cross-trained to do a variety of jobs and acquire additional skills.

FAS

The term FAS stands for Final Assembly Schedule. Final Assembly Scheduling is a method of postponement which increases efficiency and lowers costs by putting off the finishing of a product until orders are received or demand "pulls" supply.

- FAS will set times for final mixing, cutting, packaging, and other processes, which may vary from the basic product.
- The auto industry sets Final Assembly Schedules for its product "twins" like the Mercury Milan and the Ford Fusion. Such vehicles are indistinguishable from each other until they are processed for differentiation by the Final Assembly Schedule.
- The typical FAS is compiled based on customer orders received. It constrains the amounts of inventory, an excessive burden in many industries.

Types of Manufacturing

There are many different styles of manufacturing. Many facilities employ a variety of styles simultaneously. The different types of manufacturing are characterized by the direction of work flow.

- Manufacturing by lot refers to batch production. This means that a fixed number of standard finished products with fixed dates of execution are manufactured according to a contract. Since each batch is of the same stock, the lots can be given a batch number as a means of distinguishing them from other batches.
- Intermittent manufacturing moves batched lots of materials or components through an assembly or finishing facility, but each lot may pass through different work centers. The results of this type of manufacturing are batches of finished products which may vary in terms of composition and family group.
- Continuous manufacturing refers to continuous flow production (generally liquids and gases) and the type of continuous production in which solid raw materials or components follow the same path to completion.

Project and Repetitive Manufacturing Processes

Project manufacturing is preferred for large, single items like the C5A cargo aircraft, which is assembled in a hangar. Because it is large, immoveable, and packed with components, the work sequence orders and designs must be established well in advance of the operating steps.

- Project manufacturing is directed toward producing a single specialized item made up of many component parts.
- Repetitive manufacturing is preferred for the manufacture of high volumes. It is best accomplished on a flow or assembly line. Work flows through the assembly points and work centers at a fixed rate in repetitive manufacturing.
- In repetitive manufacturing, feeder lines to final assembly areas are kept fully stocked with raw materials and components; main assembly lines are loaded to a specified and finite capacity.

JIT Production

JIT is an abbreviation for "Just-In-Time" production.

- JIT means that parts or components needed for assembly lines or other manufacturing processes are provided "just in time." The Japanese concept of kanban is an integral tool in implementing JIT production.
- The materials and processes which feed and support the manufacturing process are not allowed to accumulate. Inventory does not build up. Similar to the kanban concept, ideal JIT processing delivers each part at precisely the time it is needed for manufacturing.
- JIT processing is streamlined and cost effective because it is flexible enough to meet changing demand. It does not involve extensive warehousing costs. Inventory costs can be as high as 35 percent of the total cost of production.
- JIT adds value to a product or service by decreasing the lead time from production to customer.

JIT or just-in-time production is a means of preventing unnecessary inventory from accumulating along the length of the supply line.

- Excessive inventory is costly in many ways. Aside from being "in the way" of work flows, it is often held in storage, which results in increased expenses associated with debt financing, storage space, and handling costs.
- JIT refers to the practice of limiting inventory by obtaining supplier components only when they are needed to meet production demands and schedules.
- Kanban is a technique which makes the supply chain leaner by reducing the number of parts or components moving through it to the minimum amount necessary to meet downstream demand. This lean pull from downstream can be accomplished using a variety of kanban techniques, including automated or manual (flash card) methods.
- The kanban ideal, never reached in real world operations, is to maintain only the amount of inventory necessary for the unit currently being assembled.

One of the chief advantages of kanban is that it reduces paperwork to a minimal amount. Instead of the documentation-intensive system required by Material Requirements Planning systems, kanban operations require no passage of paper from one worker to another.

- Kanban works best in manufacturing processes which have a short and fixed lead time to finished product.
- Kanban works best when demand is continuous and even flowing rather than volatile and varied.
- Kanban is effective when the constancy of demand allows for simple planning of capacity requirements.
- Kanban is well suited to mixed model production scheduling.
- Kanban works well when the component is scheduled for assembly in low order quantities.

Kanban is a method derived from the early days of Japanese auto manufacturing. It is used to signal increased demand to upstream suppliers. While the actual cards used in the original method are still used, the concept can be modified to encompass higher technology and other manufacturing tasks:

- Kanban strives for a leaner and more agile mix of components moved along the various work stations involved in the production.
- By reducing the number of components moving along the supply chain, Japanese supply chain managers are able to identify bottlenecks or other problems. While manufacturing problems are not always apparent when inventory is large, bottlenecks and other problems become apparent when excess supply is removed from inventory and buffers.
- By slimming down the assembly process, managers can more easily address the underlying issues of inefficiency in the production assembly process.

Kanban seeks to reduce the amount of inventory to the quantity needed to meet production demand. This concept is not incongruent with the traditional method of targeting economic batch order quantities (EOQ) by monitoring and manipulating ordering costs, setup costs, and inventory carrying costs.

- One rule of manufacturing is that the cost of production decreases as the economic order quantity (EOQ) improves.
- Kanban streamlines the manufacturing processes which prevent the EOQ number from declining to its ideal point of one.
- Reducing EOQ as close to the ideal point of one as possible has the result of reducing set-up costs, inventory carrying costs, and, ultimately, the total costs of production.

Implementing MRP and JIT

An MRP approach lends itself to coordinating and planning the use of materials, but it is oftentimes cumbersome on the shop floor. Equipment and work shifts are less flexible than planning concepts. There are two methods of combining JIT with MRP on the shop floor.

Use different planning and control systems for different products:

- Using the runners, repeaters, and strangers terminology, work is classified according to whether it is to be moved, repetitively produced, or separately treated.
- Standard "pull" kanbans can be scheduled for runners and repeaters.
- For "strangers," work orders are issued with specific instructions; work is monitored and "pushed" through production stages.

Use MRP for overall control and JIT for internal control.

- Use MRP for planning of supplier materials so that they are available for JIT production.
- Use MRP to break down the Master Planning Schedule to set supplier schedules in accordance with future demand.
- Kanban is used to implement JIT. All material is governed by kanban loops between operations within the factory.

Service Level Measurement

On-time delivery of quality products to the right location is one of the most important issues in continuous manufacturing. On-time delivery is necessary to meet Takt Time requirements. Late deliveries can result in costly line stops. Service level measurement is an important indicator for both the manufacturer and the supplier. Service level measurement is defined as the percentage of time that supply orders are delivered on time and in the right condition to meet demand.

The calculation for measuring service level (SL) is a comparison of the ratio between demand which is met and demand which is not met.

$$SL = \frac{(1 - Demand\ not\ Met)}{Total\ Demand} \times 100$$

Mixed Model Production

Mixed model production is a method of producing a family of products within the same scheduled production period.

Products A, B, and C, for example, may be scheduled in batch sizes of 200, 120, and 80 per week. This method of production inevitably leads to peaks and valleys in production loads. Smooth and even flows upon equipment and people operating the work centers are far more desirable.

Leveling of the schedule is a way of addressing fluctuations in production loads which impede efficiency and bottleneck the output. Leveling is scheduled to meet real-time customer demand rather than provide excessive inventory levels.

An example of basic leveling would be to reduce production of products A, B, and C to 5 of Product A, 3 of Product B, and 2 of Product C.

A thoroughly leveled mix-model method of production would refine the assembly sequence to: AABABCABCA.

Job Splitting

In an ideal world, manufacturers would have unlimited resources to invest in modern machinery. The real world requires adjustment and flexibility, especially because of the frequent purchase of unrelated parallel shop machinery, which can have different capacities and capabilities.

Capital costs, operation costs, and variability of demand may require "splitting" of jobs with a high priority and routing tasks to work stations of different capabilities.

Job "splitting" typically occurs in only two portions since larger splits would result in a counterproductively high WIP inventory.

To maintain the requisite low level of WIP inventory, the completion schedules for a two-split job should only vary within tight margins.

EFFICIENCY

APICS defines efficiency as a comparative percentage of actual output to a standard anticipated output.

- This relative efficiency is a measure of the expected outputs of any type of unit. As APICS defines efficiency, it can be a measure of efficient manufacturing output, efficient expenditure, or efficient use of time.
- If an expected standard rate of pieces produced on a flow line for a particular product is 100, and the actual result of the flow line production is only 90 pieces, then the rate of efficiency is 90%.
- Another efficiency measurement may standardize the amount of time to complete a manufacturing task, and then compare the actual time required for completion to that standard.

Successful manufacturing involves implementing efficient methods and combining those methods with concrete objectives.

- Cut WIP (work in progress) inventories.
- Cut flow times.
- Cut flow distance and space.
- Reduce the number of suppliers.
- Improve supplier performance through enhanced communication.
- Reduce parts proliferation and increase substitution possibilities.
- Design for manufacturing facility as well as customer satisfaction.
- Cross-train both managers and workers.
- Maintain accurate production, quality, and delay data.
- Seek the solutions to line flow or assembly problems through first line personnel.
- Develop and improve human expertise and resources.
- Use flexible equipment which can easily be moved from one location to another.
- Implement an incremental automation policy.

The shop floor supervisor must observe basic kanban rules in order to operate an efficient system.

- Containers must always have a move card, a production card, or both. The production cards signal downstream work centers to produce. The move card indicates that material can be moved. Taking action inconsistent with the move and production kanban cards can produce bottlenecks in production.
- Containers used in kanban must have a consistent capacity. In order for smooth materials and products flow, quantities of input and output must be standardized.
- Work sequence in kanban must always be first-in, first-out (FIFO). If work is allowed to accumulate on kanban squares while subsequent work is picked up and processed, inventory levels will accumulate to unsuitable levels.

FLEXIBILITY

Traditional make-to-stock, large-volume batch orders were proven to be far less efficient than make-to-order, smaller volume orders and flexible manufacturing practices. Flexible manufacturing can be achieved in the following ways:

- Smaller and less expensive machinery can be provided to work cells without causing the overproduction associated with large-capacity and expensive machines that have unnecessarily high volume capacities.
- The reduction of changeover times through the use of standardized machines which allow for easy conversion and setup.
- Aiming for measured machine capacity utilization rather than high capacity maximized production which produces inventory in excess of customer demand.
- Cross-training of labor adds to manufacturing flexibility by allowing more latitude in worker assignments. If each worker has expertise in several jobs, workforce numbers can be applied where needed.

Flexible manufacturing depends on being responsive in the areas of volume, labor, and new products. Manufacturing newcomers often believe that the greatest accomplishment which can be achieved is greater volume production. This is not so.

- A flow line operating at only a small percentage of capacity may be far more efficient in total measured lead time because it is consistent with customer demand, does not create excessive and expensive inventory, and does not incur high materials handling costs. This is an example of total volume flexibility.
- Product mix flexibility is geared to the needs of the customer. It also makes more efficient use of the labor force and worker expertise in different areas. Workloads are leveled in order to meet real demand rather than forecasted demand.
- New product flexibility decreases the amount of shut-down time required to re-tool and manufacture new products.

EMPLOYEES

JIT manufacturing has changed the human resource field by establishing broader criteria with respect to developing the type of personnel needed for lean manufacturing environments.

- Authority is often horizontal. Decisions are made more frequently on the work floor rather than by top-down decision making by upper management.
- Specialization has new meaning. No longer does specialization mean a narrow interest and myopic focus on a specific process. Staff specialists involved in lean JIT manufacturing must share responsibility and knowledge regarding the overall impact of the process on profitability and efficiency.
- Job rotation strategies require the labor force to master several jobs. Substitution and movement of workers within a facility adds flexibility to the production system, and also increases worker value and expertise. An outgrowth of job rotation is the concept of job enlargement, an increase in the number of tasks a worker can perform. Acquired expertise in a wider variety of areas accounts for job enrichment.

The quality of production adds as much value to manufactured items as quantity and design. It is in the interest of profitability to minimize waste and focus on a process of continuous improvement in the assembly/production process.

- Employees must be motivated to accomplish quality goals. They should strive to reach these goals as if they were co-owners of the company.
- Workers must share in the responsibility of correcting problems as they develop, and must be given the authority to do so.
- Problem-resolution teams should be cross-functional, meaning they should work across different departments.
- Communication problems can result from over-specialization of job tasks. Cross-training is a viable method of educating employees about the complex web of inter-relationships that support factory production.

An educated work force benefits a company because its workers are more loyal and also exhibit better work performance. Possibilities may vary, depending on the size of a company, but even the most under-capitalized enterprise can benefit from the variety of educational programs that may be offered.

Internal programs:

- Basic skills training can increase productivity and create a sense of pride in work accomplishment.
- Management skills training can be accomplished with management tutors.
- Plant certification can be provided to those employees who show a high degree of motivation to learn vital tasks.

External programs:

- Colleges and universities can provide training for state certification in regulatory areas. The incentive for the company is that it will be able to achieve regulatory compliance.
- Colleges can train qualified employees in highly specialized areas where it is difficult to hire staff.

Behavioral training is a general term used to refer to a variety of disciplines that can contribute to smooth operations and more efficient manufacturing firms.

- Teamwork seminars are forms of behavioral training that educate employees in cooperative work techniques.
- Management training requires a teamwork approach that emphasizes organizational success.
- Training in negotiating techniques is helpful for the leaders of many organizations. Some people do not know how to negotiate. Behavioral patterns for some people run to the extremes of submission or over-dominance. Behavioral training can teach people to work on finding a common ground, which allows for cooperative and successful information exchange.
- Training in communication skills should be provided for those individuals who have a high degree of skill or specialization, but do not know now to communicate those ideas to others.

Compensation is as much a management skill as it is an economic necessity. There are four common ways to pay personnel for the value they add to the manufacturing process.

- Incentive methods are traditional. Compensation is based on the completion of a quantity of work or the attainment of specific goals. The very old concept of "piece work" is a good example of direct, incentive-based compensation.
- Fixed rate approaches are successful only when the employees who are hired are motivated and possess the necessary skills. Fixed rate compensation is a predetermined scale of payment that is matched to job roles or production shifts. A company that pays an hourly rate or shift rate, for example, is using a fixed rate approach.

There are four common ways to pay personnel for the value they add to the manufacturing process. Incentive and fixed rate approaches are older and more traditional methods of compensation. Some companies have found they can better motivate workers through skills-based and profit-sharing approaches.

- Skills-based compensation is a way of paying employees according to the level of skill achieved. Skills-based compensation motivates employees to advance their careers by learning additional skills through the rotation of job positions and roles. In this way, their level of functioning is increased. For a floor worker, compensation might be based on changeover skills and quality control knowledge.
- Profit-sharing provides motivation because the employee's fortunes are tied to the company's profitability. Some profit-sharing programs provide regular incentive pay. Other profit-sharing programs reward meeting quality goals and lean manufacturing achievements.

Inflation of purchase estimates derives from a traditional production mindset, which sacrifices profitability to a single set of performance characteristics.

Consider the case of the material planner who wants to receive a year-end bonus for saving a company money.

- Overestimating the cost of required materials needed for a manufacturing process will generally result in a fallacious "cost savings" because purchases are actually made at less expense. Being able to say "we saved money in purchasing our materials" should not be the only criterion for the dispensation of management awards.

On-time delivery, accurate and true cost reductions, reduced inventory, and the establishment of supplier certification programs may be better alternatives when establishing criteria for performance incentives.

Many companies are struggling to revamp and update their business philosophies. Inevitably, they find that managers and workers must first be led away from the way they used to do things.

- Some managers are stuck in the traditional mold of rewarding function rather than the larger outcomes associated with profitable manufacture. A work cell in which everyone works hard may not produce any more than another one that works more efficiently, but at a leisurely pace.
- Some managers believe that the solution is more technology and expenditure, but the real answer is simplification.

- Some managers and workers are threatened by the term downsizing. The solution that can replace downsizing is right-sizing. The manufacturing cell must be designed to fit high and low peaks of demand.

ERP

Approaches to manufacturing have evolved since the days of Henry Ford's Model T assembly line. JIT production, lean manufacturing, and materials requirements planning (MRP) are reactions to increasing competition in global markets. Enterprise resource planning is a method that evolved as a response to a lack of internal integration.

- ERP is used to integrate an entire company organization into a single central operations information module. Hardware and equipment interfaces with software in order to achieve this integration. Compatibility is established throughout the centralized information system.
- ERP increases information visibility by creating a common database that can be shared by all departmental information subsystems.
- Data capture of short-term variations in an ERP database system (variations in demand, items needing rework, material costs, run times, etc.) are available to managers, who must regulate production cost accounting.
- ERP can show cause and effect relationships between different cost segments.

Little's Law

Little's Law is a set of rules developed in 1961 which measure work flow on an assembly line. The importance of Little's Law in manufacturing is in constructing a mathematical relationship between quantities of pieces, flow time in hours, and throughput in pieces per hour.

- An inventory of 1000 pieces is cumbersome and inefficient if the throughput rate is 10 pieces per hour. If the throughput rate is 500 pieces per hour, then it may be regarded as lean inventory.

The relationships between Flow Time and WIP inventory in Little's Law can be represented by:

- WIP Inventory = Throughput Rate X Flow Time
- If flow time values are needed, the following formula may be used:
- Flow time = WIP Inventory X Cycle Time

Functional and Process Layouts

Functional or traditional manufacturing layouts are centered on the machinery and equipment and include job shops and batch manufacturing. Similar processes or skills are grouped together into work centers, and products move from work center to work center to receive the necessary processing. This has been used in the past with low-volume manufacturing, but that practice is changing somewhat in the current manufacturing environment. Process layout is centered on the product itself. The process is developed and equipment placed as necessary for production of a particular item or family of items, as in line and continuous manufacturing, work cells, and group technology layouts. Process layouts are used for high volume manufacturing.

Manufacturing Lead Time

Manufacturing lead time is the total time required to manufacture a product. Here are the metrics which are part of manufacturing lead time:

- Order preparation time
- Queue time
- Setup time
- Run time
- Inspection time

In make-to-order manufacturing, manufacturing lead time is the measured block of time from the release of an order, through its production, to its shipment to the customer. Throughput time is the amount of time required for a material, part, component, or subassembly to go from the beginning to the end of the manufacturing process. It does not include ordering time, setup times, etc.

Whether the time to make a finished product is measured in terms of lead time or total elapsed time, the process must be made as efficient as possible. One of the activities which adds to the total time spent on finishing a product is the time spent moving an item or component from one work station to the next in sequence. The time spent in moving items on their way to completion does not add value to the product, but it subtracts from lead time or total elapsed time.

- A common innovation designed to eliminate move time is to link machine processes together so that the pieces do not need outside intervention to reach the next work station. This infrastructure design is the work cell or flow line.
- Another innovation intended to decrease product lead times is the use of overlapping operations. Overlapping operations sometimes adds move time, but saves queue time for those processes where the lot can be split and the subsequent stage of a process can run simultaneously.

Materials management strategies are very much impacted by predictability of demand, materials replenishment times, and product lead times.

- When product development and manufacturing lead times are long and there is a predictable, stable, and reliable supplier relationship, the amount of inventory moving from supplier to manufacturer can be lean, or reduced to a large degree. Materials and components can be brought in and manufactured according to demand.
- If product lead times are short and demand is unpredictable, a responsive or agile production process should be implemented to meet the challenge of changing demand.
- Correspondingly, if lead times are long and demand is unpredictable, production managers should emphasize lead time reduction since demand can't really be controlled.

Setup Time, Unit Run Time, Wait Time, and Move Time

All of the terms refer to manufacturing activities that are quite common and often necessary. Some add value to the product, but others do not.

Setup time refers to the adjustment which must be made to people and equipment before manufacturing can begin. Easily convertible machinery and tools designed expressly for flexible setup can aid in setup time reduction.

Unit run time may be regarded as a subdivision of the complete order cycle time. Unit run time is just one tiny segment of the order cycle time; it refers to the time required to produce a single manufactured item.

Wait time is the amount of time a product spends at a work station after that particular phase of production is complete.

Move time is another activity that does not add value to a manufactured product and must be reduced as much as possible. Move time refers to the amount of time that elapses before a product or a small batch of products moves to the queue of the next work station.

Replenishment Cycle

The replenishment cycle refers to the interface between the factory and the supplier, and to the delivery of replenishment items and products to replace depleted stock.

The manufacturer must have a replenishment plan and strategy in place that will maintain profitability and prevent machine stoppage and waste.

When replenishment triggers send information that more stock should be obtained from the supplier, the order must be placed and quickly communicated to all other affected segments of the manufacturing chain. Electronic inventory and EDI (electronic data interchange) has made this step fast and efficient.

Order fulfillment is the next step in the process cycle of replenishment. The supplier must get new stock to the manufacturer on time and at minimal cost.

The final step in replenishment is the receiving process. During the receiving process, inventory figures are updated. Money must flow from the manufacturing company to the supplier partner.

Flexible Manufacturing System

Production planners must recognize the value of flexibility in responding to changes in demand volumes and in the designing the flow routing of production channels.

- FMS stands for Flexible Manufacturing Systems. Flexible Manufacturing Systems, or FMS, are a recent and expensive development.
- Flexible Manufacturing Systems add value to products and services through the implementation of technologies which can quickly adapt to changing upstream supply and downstream demand.
- Flexible Manufacturing Systems are designed so as to have the capacity for changing and even reversing the sequences of production processes.
- A Flexible Manufacturing System will sometimes allow different machines to accomplish the same task. This capability allows for directional changes in the flow line.
- Flexible Manufacturing Systems are complex and require control by a central computer. Like the equipment itself, this type of technology expenditure can offset short-term financial indentures through long-term productivity and efficiency gains.

Cellular Manufacturing

Cellular manufacturing refers to a shop floor structural design in which machinery dedicated to a specific manufacturing task is grouped together. Machine operators within the cells are knowledgeable about all stations of that particular flow line. A cell will manufacture a single product or a group of related and very similar products. Cellular manufacturing simplifies management, leads to inventory reduction, and increases sales performance. The techniques and methods of successful cellular manufacturing require changes in approach:

- Design must be focused on customer demand concerns, not on marketing research or what internal management believes the customer should buy.
- The focus of cellular manufacturing must be realistic and specific so that the product or family of products can be delivered to the satisfaction of the customer. Focusing on too many products defeats the purpose of cellular structure.
- Command and control must be unified within the cell, and visible kanban style systems will be advantageous in achieving this.
- Machinery and equipment should be focused and dedicated to specific tasks so that setup times are negligible.
- Quality control standards must be enforced within the cell.

Cellular manufacturing combines the efficiency of product flow layouts with the flexibility of functional layouts.

- Products with similar process requirements are grouped into families and assembled in a cell of functionally dissimilar machines.
- The volume increases obtained by grouping similar products into families compensates for the dedication of equipment.
- Since volumes are justified by process and product similarity, cellular manufacturing provides more flexibility than a pure product-flow layout.
- Cellular manufacturing results in faster throughput time, better quality, lower WIP levels, and reduced set-up times. Batch sizes may therefore be reduced.
- Cell workers can collaborate in setups.
- The co-location of machinery means that batches do not have to travel very far, which leads to better floor control.

A disadvantage of cellular arrangements is that machine breakdowns may cause work stoppage in a cell. Also, the capital expense of buying dedicated equipment can only be justified by large volume output and low per-unit costs.

A simple cellular structure can be developed with relative ease in smaller companies. When giant companies attempt to adopt a cellular structure, the obstacles to doing this may seem insurmountable. The solution is to divide the corporation into smaller operating units, called focus factories. Focus factories are devoted to the manufacture of a single part, family of parts, or component units (auto transmissions, for example). Each focus factory may then be further divided into cells comprised of different machines working together to produce families of components or parts.

The focused factory concept lends itself to small business applications, but can also be implemented in large manufacturing corporations as well.

- Focus Packaging, Inc. is a single product focus factory business dedicated to making paper packaging for the huge Colgate-Palmolive Corporation.
- Focus factories are based on an economist's theory that the focused factory will out-produce, undersell, and quickly gain a competitive advantage over companies with a wider array of matters which need attention.

- The focus factory embodies an ideal of lean manufacture.
- The folding and gluing machine at Focus Packaging, Inc. requires no setup time. It produces a one size package for bar soap. It can respond quickly to orders received.

PROJECT-ORIENTED INDUSTRIES

Project-oriented industries face additional challenges with respect to making things to customer order specifications.

- Customers sometimes have control or ownership of inventory and the design process. This poses substantial challenges to accounting methods and tracking requirements.
- A project-oriented industry has additional challenges in inventory costing. Different projects may not lend themselves to the application of average costing methods.
- Cycle counting is the preferred method in project-oriented industries. The cycle count should be done at the points where the maximum benefit is obtained, which is just before major cost decisions are made and at the end of each project phase.
- Project-oriented industries take on additional responsibility since the company must be accountable to outside ownership of inventory and design processes. Waste and loss of materials may create customer problems if it is excessive and the losses impact the customer's bottom line.

QRM

QRM is the abbreviation for Quick Response Manufacturing. It was developed to address manufacturing processes which do not easily respond to JIT and kanban methods.

- QRM primarily focuses on shortening lead times throughout all components of an organization.
- QRM is most suitable for industries that manufacture specialized products in small batches that have a variety of specifications.
- QRM is also suitable for businesses that have a wide variety of demand for a wide variety of products with different specifications.
- QRM style companies do not respond as well to pull systems or kanban as they do to other inventory reduction methods.
- The objective of QRM style manufacturing is to begin building the product after the orders are received.

The batch and queue method of old style manufacture is subject to large bottlenecks and frequent stoppages. This style of production is rapidly being replaced by lean production, which minimizes inventory buildup.

- QRM is one style of cellular flow line production. It is different from other similar forms in that the direction of flow is not always the same.
- QRM design is such that takt time, level scheduling, and flex fences are measured and used as a basis for designing the individual phases of work within each cell.
- QRM line processes depend on flexibility since the objective is to manufacture a wide variety of products that have a great variability of demand.

While efficient administration of QRM processes lowers inventory, QRM does not focus so much on inventory reduction as do the kanban techniques associated with JIT production.

- JIT production strives to eliminate waste as a means of continuously improving the process. QRM lead time reduction processes also result in elimination of waste, which is a natural consequence of the process.
- JIT production measures primary performance characteristics, such as on time delivery.
- QRM consistently measures lead times. In QRM, shrinking lead times results in on-time delivery. The key difference is on matters of focus or emphasis to achieve results.
- JIT flow lines are designed in such a way as to expedite continuous movement of a single product without inventory buildup or bottleneck stoppages. QRM flow line design is non-linear, and products can take different paths through the cell. The cells for QRM are designed to accommodate the specific products to be manufactured, rather than with the aim of achieving a smooth, linear flow.
- QRM methods utilize flexibility to meet varying demand for a wide variety of products. QRM systems take advantage of techniques like time-slicing and a better understanding of system dynamics to reach production targets. JIT lean flow line manufacturing uses the techniques of takt time and level scheduling as the primary means of control.
- In lean manufacturing, JIT and kanban techniques are combined to match demand curves to production flows. Flex fences and pull signals characterize JIT lean manufacturing. QRM industries rely on suppliers to match their operations to the manufacturing customer work flow needs.
- QRM does not begin production until an order arrives at the manufacturer. QRM uses POLCA, a combination of push and pull flow line operation, to prevent bottlenecks and work stoppages. JIT uses kanban, often termed a "ship one – make one" process, to meet demand. JIT pull methods do not work for complex and customized manufacturing processes for products with a variety of specifications.

The choice of a suitable manufacturing process structure will depend on the customer segment to be served.

- QRM is the better choice when the customer needs custom-engineered items designed with a wide variety of options. JIT lean manufacturing with linear flow lines employing kanban pull systems are suitable for baseline products, which do not have significant product variation.
- QRM is ideal for companies seeking new market niches, which often have unpredictable and widely varying demand. JIT lean manufacturing is best for manufacturing consumer products that require continuous replenishment and have a stable demand.

Eliminating the response time spiral is a major step in Quick Response Manufacturing. The response time spiral is based on single-function, lower cost production, which ignores all other relevant activities that would reduce lead time.

- QRM is not as simple as speeding up existing operations. It depends on new approaches to completing the same job in a way that will reduce lead times.
- QRM may require a re-design of the organization and management structure, which will result in time-saving methodology rather than reactive cost-cutting.

- QRM aims at reducing leading times from the point the order is received until the order ships to the customer. It focuses on every facet or segment of the production process: sales, order entry, engineering, production planning, testing, packaging, transportation, fabrication, and assembly.

Supply Chain Management

The traditional approach to manufacturing has been a logistics approach. Logistics focuses strictly on moving materials: the methods of moving it and the time it takes for delivery. A weakness of this approach is that it does not take inventory levels into account. Logistics approaches often suffer from too much supply or too little supply. This weakness led to the development of supply chain management.

- Supply chain management puts the spotlight on areas of materials acquisition which add value to the entire manufacturing process. Adding value through better materials management means higher quality products at more competitive prices.
- SCM evaluates all steps in materials acquisition and delivery and makes adjustments which focus on delivery reliability, leaner inventories, and positive, rapid communication between factories and suppliers.

Throughput Efficiency

Throughput efficiency is the percentage value of the time in the production process which adds to product value compared to the percentage value of time in the production process which does not.

- It has been estimated that raw materials move through a system of manufacture with a throughput efficiency of only ten percent. Obviously, company profits can be greatly increased by the achievement of higher throughput efficiency.
- Better management of throughput efficiency will lead to lower costs, higher quality, and a more rapid response to customer demand. Yet, a great deal of production time is consumed by activity which adds no value to the product.
- Throughput efficiency can be calculated by dividing the amount of Value Added Time by the End to End Pipeline Time and multiplying by 100 percent.

$$Throughput = Value\ Added\ Time \div End\ to\ End\ Pipeline\ Time \times 100\%$$

- Throughput efficiency can be increased by eliminating or minimizing the amount of time a product spends in the pipeline without value being added.
- Flexible manufacturing systems can diminish excessive setup and changeover times when new product manufacturing begins.
- Kanban can prevent bottlenecks in the flow of materials and thwart unnecessary and costly inventory buildup.
- The introduction of better visibility into the production pipeline will improve communication and coordination throughout all phases of assembly.

PRODUCTION SCHEDULING

The establishment of a production schedule requires cooperation and communication across different operating segments.

- Scheduling factory production begins with the production plan established at the sales and operations planning meeting.
- Master schedulers segment the production plan into daily or weekly production schedules. The most efficient schedules consist of family groups which use common materials and components.
- MRP then develops low level manufacturing schedules and organizes the purchase of components that must be ordered.
- Order scheduling is done by Material Requirements Planners.
- Detailed scheduling is accomplished at the CRP (capacity requirements level) or at the PAC (Production Activities Control) level.

The operations schedule determines the timing and manner in which resources within a factory are used. The operations method relates to the sequence in which various operations are scheduled. These short-term, separately-scheduled operations should be consistent with long-term production goals in terms of quantity and completion date. The overall goal is always efficient use of labor, equipment, and materials.

- The operations schedule sets start and completion dates consistent with expected customer delivery dates.
- The operations schedule assures that quantity and volume goals are consistent with customer demand.
- The operations schedule sequences work according to a set of planning priorities.
- The operations schedule is vital to product families which follow different and often complex assembly paths because of size, color, or other design characteristics.

Operation schedule is derived from production planning group activity, which is essentially an estimate or "rough-cut" projection of the operating schedule.

- An operation schedule states the quantities, completion dates, configurations, and work center groups involved, and the number of hours required for setup and run times.
- Operation schedules must consider backlogs of items planned, released, and begun.
- Operation schedules must determine material availability, the amount of inventory, material from suppliers, and sub-production from component producers.
- Operation schedules must determine capacity and the work centers which will be involved in production.
- Operation schedules must also account for move times, which is the amount of time spent moving an unfinished product from one work center to another.

Scheduling Factory Production

Manufacturing changes mean that manufacturing is becoming increasingly more competitive. What worked five years ago may be irrelevant today because technology is constantly changing the capabilities of product manufacture.

- Mindsets should not be locked into the traditional. As with all manufacturing processes, mindsets should be responsive, fluid, and flexible.
- Manufacturing a product in specified amounts even though orders have significantly and consistently diminished is a common mistake.
- If the diminished number of orders stems from cyclical demand cycles, then production should be rescheduled and adjusted according to seasonal changes in demand or other fluctuations.
- Should the demand decrease be attributed to obsolescence, the manufacture of those obsolete products should stop, and that production should be entirely removed from the master planning schedule.

Production Sequencing

A team-based approach to production sequencing relies on providing the Master Production Schedule to each work team.

- Sequentially number each production order in the MPS horizon.
- Instead of sorting by end item, this approach requires that orders be sorted by due date. Orders that have the same due date are grouped together.
- Each cell, work center, or department is marked with a set of inbound and outbound kanban squares on the shop floor.
- The work sequence on the front end is the same sequence that flows downstream to the next cell or work station.
- Production sequencing is an efficient way of using a pull system to move customer orders to completion in a make-to-order style of job shop.
-

Synchronized Manufacturing Process

Synchronicity in manufacturing refers to the simultaneous management and coordination of all component production elements. Synchronization of the production line is necessary in order to prevent bottlenecks, unnecessary inventory, and unresponsive product manufacturing.

- Strategies must be developed which will permit material movement and positioning, scheduling of production, forecasting of demand, and capacity management.
- Design components and equipment positioning support the smooth flow of product through each step of the manufacturing process. Material handling should be minimized. Electrical and mechanical configurations must be flexible.
- Introduction of new products must allow for testing, prototyping, and design validation.
- Order management must be conducted to enable production report capture, order tracking, and error management.
- The process alignment which must accompany supply chain synchronization involves a high level of collaboration and coordination between operational levels.

SMED and FMS

Competitive manufacturing practices require that the customer's needs be met in ever shorter lead times. In order to achieve a quick response (QR) to demand, the production managers can draw from single minute exchange of die (SMED) and flexible manufacturing systems (FMS).

- FMS involves designing the production process with a view to flexibility. FMS, or flexible manufacturing systems, refers to the ability to quickly change the amount of produced items and the ability to produce variations of a specific product.
- The Japanese innovation of SMED (single minute exchange of die) is focused on reducing set-up times through analyzing the process and improving the process with technology and better application of human resources.

Pipeline Management

Pipeline management is not a single goal; it is a series of goals. Desired outcomes of supply chain management include:

- Lower costs
- Higher quality
- Flexible manufacturing schedules
- Rapid response to customer demand

Achieving these goals creates value. Yet, a large part of the production schedule consumes time without adding value to the product. The comparison and measurement of time which adds value and time which doesn't add value is called throughput efficiency.

It is estimated that raw materials move through an industrial system of manufacture from end to end with a throughput efficiency of only ten percent. Obviously, that leaves a great deal of room for improvement for production management.

Mixed-Model Production

Mixed model production is the process of manufacturing different product models on the same assembly line. The process sets specific output rates for upstream suppliers to create a smooth flow rate.

- Mixed-model production stabilizes the demand on upstream suppliers who provide components or parts to an assembly line operation.
- Mixed-model production may have multiple tributaries, but products flow from supplier to user at the pace which matches the needs of downstream suppliers. One tributary may send three components downstream each hour, while another supply stream may be set to send four components each hour to meet the needs of downstream assembly.
- Mixed model production does not require changeovers or refitting of equipment and machinery.
- Mixed model production stabilizes labor requirements.

Each type of manufacturing has its own unique problems which must be addressed in order for the system to function properly. The problems often encountered with mixed-model assembly are:

- Flexibility issues: These can be addressed by ensuring that workers within the same area share skills and work backlogs. The allowance of small quantity inventories between work stations allows for flexibility of operation. Work content must be the same for each work station in order to maintain work balance.

- Parts availability is a common problem which can be alleviated by the employment of small scale kanban techniques.
- Availability of tools: This can be addressed by creating standardized outfitting of tool stations. Multi-purpose tools can be useful, provided such tools are properly designed and appropriate to the type of assembly being produced.

OMP

Operations Management Planning occurs after top management has created a general plan for sales and operations, business planning, and resource requirements. This phase of planning involves translating the initial phase production planning into item numbers and dates of manufacture. Operations Management Planning (the mid-level of MPC) consists of:

- Rough-Cut Capacity Planning should establish maximum production capacity and maximum material and labor capacity.
- Materials Requirements Planning sets the stage for the production schedule.
- Master Production Scheduling should set the parameters for manufacturing the product, from raw material to finished product.
- Distribution Planning is vital to Operations Management Planning, and assures that materials will be available to meet production schedules.

Production Plan

A key point to remember about production plans set by senior management is that they must contain signatures authorizing operations personnel to act. Organizing the purchase of materials and supplying equipment and human resources is no small task for any organization.

- The production plan matches resources to requirements for current and future periods. Anticipated availability and the cost of raw materials are considered, and adjustment scenarios are developed.
- Shipping schedules are set according to product families. The types of items and the quantities that will be shipped are also determined.
- The rate of production is set in accordance with projected sales, which is calculated based on market research figures.
- Current and future inventory levels are assessed in terms of storage, pilferage, and distribution costs.

Planning Cycle

Sales and operations segments meet regularly to identify the needs of the organization and changing circumstances. Among the issues which are addressed and discussed at regular planning meetings are:

- Inventory levels
- Seasonal changes in production and sales
- Disparities between forecasted sales figures and actual sales figures
- Product grouping and differentiation: Similar items are manufactured at the same time to improve efficiency. For example, a group of cleaning agents might be manufactured together, but this family group wouldn't include a much different product like lipstick.
- Monthly and quarterly production scheduling: Monthly scheduling covers the timeline of the master production schedule, including the cumulative lead time and the batching period. Quarterly schedules are set for the remainder of the time.

Manufacturing, Remanufacturing, and Repair

There are key differences between manufacturing, remanufacturing, and repair.

- In repair, only the worn parts or the parts which have completely failed are replaced.
- In remanufacturing, nearly all working parts are restored to original, like-new condition.
- In manufacturing, all finished products derive from raw materials and components.
- The most fundamental differences are related to material control functions:
- In remanufacture, the available materials are unknown until disassembly.
- In standard manufacturing, the availability of raw materials and components is known by consulting the build schedule.
- Examples of remanufacturing can be drawn from the fields of auto components or computers.
- Many computer makers sell both new and refurbished computers. While refurbished computers or other electronics are less expensive, they typically offer similar guarantees.
- Auto engines and parts like generators or fuel injection systems are frequently rebuilt. Because of the high cost of more complex auto component systems, profits can be significant.

Globalization

Globalization requires adaptation to new conditions in the marketplace. The longer supply chains of international markets present new challenges to industry.

- The global pipeline has legal, financial, and national boundaries, which require thorough examination, planning, and revision.
- Globalization requires interface and coordination with third party components manufacturers, distributors, and after-market services located around the world.
- While globalization gives companies the advantage of lower labor costs, it offers new management challenges. The lengthening of the supply lines, language barriers, and diverse legal environments can lengthen lead times to such a degree that heavy financial losses occur.
- Short product life cycles require that global supply chains be efficiently monitored and managed over the complex web of suppliers, distributors, manufacturers, and sales operations involved in global markets.

Globalization of industry has necessitated the development of improved communication channels.

- The Internet and extranet have made it possible to provide easy access to prices, availability of material, delivery dates, credit balances, notifications of product line changes, and other relevant data.
- Many countries have developed their technology infrastructure to keep up with that used in the United States, but other countries may be limited in EDI (electronic data interchange). Pitfalls in this area have continued to confound some enterprises.
- A significant improvement in communicating material requirements to suppliers has been the electronic distribution of supplier manuals. It is a distinct advantage that information regarding purchase processes, importation documents, and delivery information is readily accessible.
- Editing, organization, and revision of vital documents, templates, and other instructional materials is easier to implement, and can be maintained at a considerable cost savings.

Contract Provisions

Search engines offer many different ways of looking for needed manufacturing data. Information sharing, employee educational resources, and cost saving are currently available and immediately accessible. The Internet has made it easier to locate important information that was once contained in old-fashioned paper manuals.

- Contracts must provide specific protections for all parties involved in a business transaction.
- Contracts must spell out rules, policies, and regulations that apply to the negotiation of contract disputes.
- Contracts must provide protection of trademark and brand territory.
- Contracts must spell out the protocol to be observed if the contract execution date is so extended as to impair the operation of the trading partner.
- Contracts must be egalitarian so that they will lead to enduring, cooperative business relationships, rather than adversarial ones.

Process Mapping Techniques

Process mapping can be applied to many administrative procedures to gain an advantage in productivity. Administrative procedures have a powerful impact on factory production.

Applying process mapping techniques can result in cost savings, better throughput, and higher levels of profitability.

Administrative processes can be streamlined by process mapping.

Process mapping consists of a series of steps:

- Determine the issues to be resolved and the specific performance metrics which need improvement.
- Chart the relationships among various levels of the organization with a view to exposing disconnects or weaknesses in cooperative management.
- Eliminate duplicated processes and levels of authority.
- Construct a sequential functional map of processes and identify any areas of weak relationship.
- Isolate and communicate to other team members the areas where the greatest performance enhancements can be achieved. Assign teams of "experts" to each area.

Process Oriented Flows

The objective of process oriented flows is to convert functional machines into a series of processes based on family groups. Process-oriented flows reduce travel distance, floor space, and throughput times. One piece is worked at a time, as opposed to an entire batch. Some caution is necessary, however.

When volume is high and flow is continuous, small variances can develop into large variances. These variances run the risk of becoming prolonged if upstream quality control problems are neglected.

Continuous process-oriented flow lines require close monitoring of back flushing activity.

In continuous process-oriented flow, it may not be possible to monitor every activity. It is more feasible to monitor activity at checkpoints or milestone points in order to identify deficiencies in upstream activity.

Cost of Facility Layouts

The general categories of facility layouts are the process layout, the cell layout, the product layout, and a mixed combination of layouts. Cost research data indicates the degree of cost associated with each type of infrastructure layout.

- The project approach to manufacturing is a type of manufacturing which uses a fixed position to build large "projects" like boats or cargo planes, or large, "one-off" pieces of equipment. This type of manufacturing has the highest cost.
- The second most costly manufacturing layout, according to statistics, is the process layout.
- The cell layout is more cost efficient than the previous methods, and is better suited to higher volume, lower variability manufacturing.
- Least expensive of all is the product layout. The product layout is similar to traditional assembly line production with lean-style modifications. Product layouts are effective when used to assemble high volume, low variability products.

Capacity Management

Capacity management is a primary goal of a production planning and control system. Capacity management involves the use of several techniques:

- Resource Requirements Planning (RRP)
- Rough-Cut Capacity Planning (RCCP)
- Capacity Requirements Planning (CRP)
- Input/Output Control

The logic system of MRP aims to determine whether there are shortages or excesses in the manufacturing system. All of the above components employ a logic system which will match orders to the capacity to produce items consistent with the Master Planning Schedule.

Equivalent Unit of Production

An equivalent unit of production is a term used in process costing. A selected time period is measured and costs are averaged for the number of units produced during that time period.

- Equivalent unit of production is a means of measuring the cost of a manufacturing activity using a common denominator. The method ascribes a unit value to items in various stages of manufacture. An item in the WIP stage of manufacture is assigned an arbitrary equivalent unit of 0.5, for example.

A formula can then be applied:

- Units produced = Closing WIP + Completed Units – Opening WIP

Keep in mind that, when using this method, WIP inventory is typically counted at one-half a unit. For example, 1000 items in WIP would have a unit equivalent value of 500.

Capacity Planning

Capacity planning is needed to ensure that the manufacturing capabilities of all combined work centers are accurately matched to the levels of planned production. Capacity planning occurs in three stages:

- Overall resource planning is conducted in accordance with the rough-cut capacity plans outlined in the master production schedule. At this early level, it is not feasible to apply material supply to machine capacity because too detailed an approach would diminish the freedom to adjust capacities in later stages.
- Second stage capacity planning is based on detailed material requirements.
- Final stage capacity planning consists of an input and output analysis based on the degree to which capacity can adjust to upstream material supply and downstream demand. Input instructions are specific, and capacity is accurately matched to machinery and equipment.

Production Activity Control

Production Activity Control is responsible for meeting planned production output levels required of manufacturing schedules. The major functions of PAC are:

- Work scheduling that is consistent with the production schedules set by master planners.
- Work loading, which not only provides the components and raw materials needed for assembly, but also provides the documentation, assembly instructions, routing documents, and the stores' picking lists.
- Systems for tracking WIP (work in progress).
- A system of recordkeeping which includes payroll data, worker hours and attendance, and status reporting.
- A communications dispatch system capable of delivering effective production schedule management,
- Production status reports, which should provide information regarding work station efficiency, capacity utilization, and reports of delayed production activities,

Authorizing Management Personnel

Very little can happen in the way of manufacturing until manufacturing activity is authorized. Authorization of manufacturing activity acts as a portal from which all activity flows. Unseen from the factory floor is the company's financing and cash flow management, which must support factory operations.

- Material, labor, and equipment must be authorized.
- Sequencing plans, routing sheets, and lot orders must be authorized before manufacturing can begin.
- Before manufacturing is authorized, the planners must review the availability of labor, materials, and equipment. They must also ensure there is appropriate accompanying documentation.
- Manufacturing orders must be examined for accuracy before the work pack is passed along to the floor foreman.

Drum-Buffer-Rope

The drum-buffer-rope approach is a way of managing supply, production, and distribution according to a theory of constraints model. It is a technique developed to thwart, halt, or diminish the inevitable bottlenecks which occur in supply and production channels.

- In traditional distribution channels, each component of the production system views itself as an independent entity. Such traditional systems work well enough initially, but, as time goes by, backlogs of unfilled orders accumulate, stockouts occur, and orders tend to increase.
- Increasing orders and large backlogs create huge production demands, which cause an over-reaction followed by an over-supply.
- The drum-buffer-rope system imposes a constraint that prevents this from happening. A buffer is used, the size of which is adjusted based on capacity differences between different work stations or components of the production chain.

MPS

MPS is the abbreviation for Master Production Scheduling. APICS defines a Master Production Schedule as a set of figures and projections used as the basis for materials requirements planning.

- Unlike forecast data, the Master Production Schedule is specific with respect to the configuration of product groups to be manufactured, the quantities to be manufactured, and the target dates for beginning and completion.
- The MPS takes into account the demand forecast figures, as well as other, more volatile areas such as availability of material and management policies.
- Within the process of developing a Master Production Schedule, management teams will integrate historic demand figures with forecasts of both trend variation and seasonality. Standing inventory and "pipeline" inventory will also be considered.

While any Master Production Schedule must be tailored to fit the needs of a particular company, all Master Production Schedules have several characteristics in common:

- Successful manufacturing requires a forward time plan for the manufacture and assembly of major components and/or finished products.
- The MPS assures that modular components are available for completion of the final assembly process.
- The MPS serves a vital function in that it serves as the basis for the manufacture of piece items and lower level manufacture.
- The MPS is used for rough-cut capacity planning by the master scheduler. Rough-cut capacity planning assures that the workload is balanced across the entire factory assembly process.
- The MPS advances the "available to promise" inventory. The available to promise inventory is the amount of stock that can be delivered to the customer within a specific time frame.

Master Production Scheduling must be a stable process if it is to support overall efficiency and profitability. Among the guidelines which should be followed are:

- Establishing a stable, lower level schedule supports finished product assembly.
- Time frames must be secure and fixed in order to guarantee an organized manufacturing process.
- Control of the Master Production Schedule requires that orders loaded into the system be consistent with cumulative lead times and firm order quantities.
- A capacity for change which recognizes capacity and material availability is crucial.

- A buffering system of safety stock is necessary to compensate for temporary lapses in demand forecasting.
- There must be realistic adherence to capacity requirements which will not overload the system and lead to unfinished products in the pipeline.

SALB

Simple assembly line balancing consists of moving work pieces along a material handling device (such as a conveyor belt) in such a way that individual operations are performed with the greatest degree of efficiency.

- A batch of raw material components moves along to the next work station, whereupon another subsequent set of assembly operations (a task) is launched.
- The time span between operations is referred to as cycle time.
- Assembly line balancing consists of optimally balancing the assembly tasks among all stations so that finished product schedules are met and the product is ready for delivery.
- Tasks are single units of work which cannot be further broken down. Therefore, each task has a processing time or task time.
- Due to practical limitations, tasks cannot be carried out in arbitrary sequence. Each task must have a pre-set priority in order to accomplish the finishing objective. For example, objects cannot be scheduled for a painting task and then for a subsequent sanding task because that would remove the paint applied earlier.

Assembly Lines

The most traditional and simple assembly line is the serial line. In this configuration, the work travels along a more or less straight path down through its various assembly stages or tasks.

The U-shaped assembly line forms the work stations into a narrow, U-shaped configuration. There is an advantage in arranging both legs of the "U" together, and it is that additional work stations may be interposed between the legs of the "U." These stations are generally termed crossover stations. Crossover stations allow for the work to return to a previous station without changing the overall line flow.

A paced assembly line assures that all operations can proceed at the scheduled rate of production.

- In Simple Assembly Line Balancing, the cycle time of all stations must be the same; otherwise, there will be bottlenecks and waiting periods.
- Assembly line balancing should be such that all work stations have the same cycle time. This is called a paced assembly line.
- A proper line balance assigns tasks to work stations without ever violating a precedence relationship.
- Some work station times can be shorter than the cycle time set for the assembly line. The idle time resulting from a shortened cycle time at a particular work station must be calculated when evaluating production cost and efficiency.
- The idle time factor must be minimal at all work stations.

Mixed-Model Assembly Lines

Single-model assembly lines are the easiest to design for maximum efficiency, but modern production lines are more often mixed-model types. These are capable of simultaneously producing a number of various products. There are two distinct types of mixed-model production.

- A mixed-model line can produce different model units in an arbitrarily mixed sequence as long as precedence violations do not occur. Such an assembly chain must be designed so as to reduce line stoppages, utility work, or off-line repair. The balancing and sequencing problem is based on an average model-to-mix ratio. This method of standardization, called horizontal balancing, has the objective of equalizing the work content of all stations over all models.
- A multi-model line produces in a sequence of batches. Each batch contains largely identical items. The items do not vary enough to significantly decrease production capacities and efficiencies.

Line Control

Assembly line control can be categorized according to the manner in which movement is controlled between work stations. The type of line control has an impact on the type of line balancing which is employed.

- Paced assembly line systems are those where each work station is set to a fixed time value. The cycle time is the same for all stations; therefore, they transfer work at the same rate.
- Unpaced assembly lines are those in which work products are not required to wait through an established cycle time before being transferred to another work station.
- Synchronous unpaced assembly lines are those in which work pieces are moved only after all work stations have completed their operations. Work stations that finish their processes early hold their products until the stations with the highest work contents have finished their production task.
- Asynchronous unpaced assembly lines are those where unfinished products are moved to available stations as soon as the task is finished. This can only happen if the succeeding station does not block the transfer by not having completed its own task.

Cycle Time Measurement

Cycle time is the length of time necessary to carry out a single process transaction. By reducing cycle times, companies can increase capacity, eliminate waste, improve quality, and improve customer satisfaction.

Cycle time is different from run time. Run time is a subcategory of cycle time, and refers to the time actually spent in completing a specific task. Run time does not include categories like setup, whereas cycle time can include activities not included in run time.

- One way of measuring cycle time is to use receipt to receipt time, which includes queue time and downtime. This method, however, has its drawbacks. It is not an effective way to estimate cycle times for future products because it is not accurate unless all single units produced are measured and used as a guide.
- Another method is to measure WIP and divide that figure by the pack calculation. Pack figures are easy to obtain because they are needed in financial accounting offices. Monthly pack figures are divided by the number of days in the month to get the daily figure.

Two chief ways of reducing cycle times are by increasing throughput or decreasing the amount of WIP. WIP depends heavily on lot size. There are instances in which reducing lot size will result in a decreased WIP.

- Some processes quickly experience a throughput increase due to the simple act of reducing lot sizes.
- Smaller lot sizes are beneficial if there are quality problems, material shortages, or demand changes which require a flow line response or complete abandonment of a production run. Reducing quality deficiencies thereby has the effect of increasing throughput.
- Multi-product flow lines may not benefit from lot size and WIP reduction. Multi-product flow lines require additional setup time. If the amount of additional setup time is larger than the time gained from faster throughput of smaller batch sizes, there will be no overall gain in productivity.

BOTTLENECKS

APICS defines a bottleneck as a facility, function, department, or resource whose capacity is less than the demand placed upon it. Prevention strategies include:

- Schedule breaks and lunch periods so that machines can continuously operate by having alternate staff on duty.
- All preparation work must be done in advance of the previous task sequence reaching the work station.
- Assess the capabilities of equipment operators to determine whether machine and conveyor belt activity speeds may be increased.
- Consider the possibility of sub-contracting repetitive simple work steps if the elimination of a step can be accomplished by high-volume, low-cost subcontracting methods.
- Troubleshoot specific problems if bottlenecks consistently occur at a single workstation.
- Machine or equipment breakdowns must always be treated as a top priority.

An assembly or manufacturing process consists of several work stations.

- For a multiplicity of reasons, some work stations will be performing efficiently and at near 100% capacity, while others are not. To compensate for this irregularity between fully-productive work stations and others that are backlogged or bottlenecked, the materials planners set a particularly sized buffer in place, which can be neither too large nor too small.
- While the non-bottlenecked station has completed its production, the bottlenecked station begins to consume the materials held in the buffer.
- The production rate (or drumbeat) is set so that the spare capacity of the non-bottlenecked station is used to maintain the size of the buffer set before the bottlenecked station.

BOTTLENECK CONTROL PLAN

It is important to have a bottleneck control plan to fall back on when bottlenecks occur. Congestion in the assembly line can hurt profitability by increasing overall cycle times.

A bottleneck can be caused either by the process or by machines, which includes failures in information technology.

- Tight control of production must be linked to demand visibility at the output end of the manufacturing process. Kanban techniques can provide visibility in the downstream segments of the manufacturing chain.
- Flow line managers can lessen the chances of bottlenecks by reducing set-up times and the number of set-ups required, and by streamlining the information flow throughout all steps of the assembly process.
- Eliminate non-productive or downtime at the bottleneck. Schedule alternatives during lunch time and breaks.

TOC

Theory of Constraints (TOC) is a concept which recognizes that most production problems occur as the result of going outside the boundaries of inherent limitations within a process.

- An example of a constraint would be implementing a production process that would require twenty machines in a facility containing only ten machines.
- The theory of constraints is a measure designed to fix existing constraints within a production system that are causing inefficient production.
- The theory of constraints system is designed to counteract constraints by establishing buffers designed to match capacity or supply differences.
- The TOC also focuses on reducing cycle times by eliminating steps in the production process that do not add value to the finished product.

The theory of constraints (or TOC) can succeed in minimizing or eliminating many of the problems encountered in factory production. It relies on a series of steps:

- The first step in implementing TOC is to identify the production constraint. Is the location of the raw materials supply the problem? Is it an employee problem? Is it a machine capacity problem?
- Exploit the constraint: This may seem counter-intuitive, but instead of overreacting, weaknesses in production can be exploited without adding expensive resources or new capacity. Can opening the communication lines with over-stressed workers help resolve the problem?
- Elevate the constraint by re-routing work or subcontracting.
- Adopt a policy of continuous improvement. Apply the Pareto Principle (the 80-20 rule) to address the eighty percent of issues which cause the greatest amount of production inefficiency.

An example of the Theory of Constraints approach in a typical through-put operation would be:

- Identifying the problem: In this example, the management was using incorrect productivity numbers. Machine human operator time was measured instead of continuous machine operating time. Machine availability was at the heart of this constraint.
- Exploiting the constraint consists of establishing a baseline system of 100% capacity utilization with daily and monthly recording of machine operator production.
- Subordinate all aspects of production to meet realistic and high productivity through-put goals. For example, the response should be that labor would be increased subordinate to machine availability.

- Elevate the constraint by removing special conditions caused by work shift constraints. For example, there may be problems staffing a particular shift, which can be remedied by moving time-consuming tasks to shifts more fully staffed.
- Continuous improvement involves recognizing and rewarding the efforts of improvement teams.

The TOC is sometimes known as a drum-buffer-rope system because the Theory of Constraints and the drum-buffer-rope system are both ways of dealing with bottlenecks, slack time, and other recurrent problems in assembly manufacturing and other activities. The TOC resolution is to use three concrete symbols (drum, buffer, rope) to represent different production activities.

- Drum refers to drumbeat. A drumbeat is the pace of work, the pace of production, and the rate at which all activities must occur in order to prevent bottleneck conditions.
- Buffer refers to the pre-set amount of materials that must be maintained as work progresses from raw materials or components through a number of assembly or finishing stations to a completed product.
- Rope is the symbol for the communications which must exist from supply portal to finished product. The flow of product and manufacturing must be consistent and manageable.

Off-Line Repair

Off-line repair is just one of the strategies available to correct assembly and manufacturing problems, which result in defective merchandise.

- The off-line repair method requires the assembly worker to remove the part from the line and begin to work on the next part.
- Removing the part from the main flow line has the advantages of no line disruptions and no loss of output, in contrast to the "stop-line method" often employed in Japanese manufacturing. A disadvantage of off-line repair is that it produces higher levels of scrap.
- Defective parts or components are moved to a separately maintained repair shop unattached to main flow lines.
- Off-line repair shop workers determine whether the defect should be repaired or scrapped.
- Parts needing major repair are disassembled and reassembled.
- Off-line repair shops require expensive extra workers, extra shifts, floor space, and equipment. Accounting practice is to classify such expenditures as sunk costs.

On-Line Repair

On-line repair is sometimes called "stop-line," because that's what most often happens. The assembly conveyance is stopped. Some of the other activities that occur as a result of the stoppage include:

- Getting outside help from a help team, which may consist of workers from adjacent or idle stations, engineers, or even the maintenance crew is usually part of the process.
- If a problem or defect is minor and not severe enough to stop the line, the worker may signal others on the line with a yellow signal light. A red light is the signal for a complete line stop.
- When major defects are noted, the line stop should occur when the impact on other processes is minimal. The only exception is when there is a safety concern.
- The help team arrives at the work center to troubleshoot the problem. The time, duration, location, and cause of the stoppage will be recorded in the interest of minimizing future stoppages.

- Online repair strategies require an investment in stop buttons, sensors, signaling devices, and other technology.
- The formation of help teams with sufficient expertise is a primary concern.

Block Scheduling

Standardized task times are a great help in scheduling and in balancing the assembly line. However, there are times when stochastic task times are too unreliable. Another alternative is to use block scheduling.

- Block scheduling views the workload as a series of individual tasks that occupy blocks of time.
- Each production batch is broken down into component activity segments: stores picking, metal stamping, pressing, milling, drilling, polishing, etc.
- A set amount of time is established for each block segment.
- The overall job is then scheduled through the entire factory, with different operations assigned.

Block scheduling is viewed in some quarters as an outmoded approach to efficient manufacturing. Because planning and scheduling are so generalized, lead time projections are either overly optimistic or are so generous that they account for lower production.

Manufacturing Measurement

Managers of manufacturing activities must be judicious in choosing points of measurement. Measurement must be directed toward meeting customer demand and company objectives, rather than toward isolated objectives, such as maximizing equipment utilization.

- A common error in measurement is choosing an outlook that is too narrow. Focusing the measurement capacity on single points like machine utilization can hamper the company's profitability.
- The result of focusing on equipment utilization would be that the machine operator would believe he/she would be rewarded for running the equipment continuously, rather than in a way that accommodates demand.
- Continuous running of equipment when it is not needed results in equipment wear expenses and excess inventory.
- Worker resources could be better applied to other areas where backlogs mean additional workers are required.

Evaluating Manufacturing Performance

It is important to monitor and measure a variety of activities to ensure a high quality and timely manufacturing output.

Measurement of Performance, in comparison to production plans, is the amount of product actually built divided by the number of products scheduled to be assembled. It is vital to determine, measure, and document the reasons for any delays in scheduling. Equipment failures require different management action than do inventory problems.

Routing Accuracy is a major source of problems, and can be measured to determine the causes of the largest problems. Accepted minimums are 95%, but it is the foolish manager who stops there.

Factory performance has a large impact on sales and customer satisfaction. It is important to monitor a variety of inputs to ensure high quality and a timely output.

- Bill of Material Accuracy standards set the minimum acceptable level at 98%. Inaccurate quantities or units of measure on a single level will corrupt the entire parent level.
- Inventory Record Accuracy measures the percentage of time inventory is in the right place in the correct amounts. The minimum acceptable level for this is 95%.
- Performance Sales Accuracy compares the number of finished products actually sold to the number that was estimated to sell. The reason for any variance must be determined. Selling less than the projected number could be due to an error in demand estimates, or it could be caused by delayed production, for example.
- Measurement of Performance, in comparison to production plans, is the amount of product actually built divided by the number of products scheduled to be assembled. It is vital to determine, measure, and document the reasons for any delays in scheduling. Equipment failures require different management action than do inventory problems.
- Routing Accuracy is a major source of problems, and can be measured to determine the causes of the largest problems. Accepted minimums are 95%, but it is the foolish manager who stops there.

Taking the myopic view of increasing production volume may make certain numbers look good, but it does not add to shareholder value if demand falls off or if technology changes. It is always wise to link manufacturing processes to customer-based measurement.

- Evaluate the market to determine the specific customer expectations of demand and desired service level.
- Base performance metrics on functional elements like order turnaround time or set-up time reduction.
- Use time-to-market and time-to-volume measurements as a way of assessing the firm's ability to respond to demand.
- Measure percentages of customer orders shipped on promised dates.
- Measure percentages of customer orders against standard market delivery lead times, even if promised dates are met. If competitors are shipping with shorter lead times, an adjustment is needed to prevent market share loss.

Product Positioning Strategies

Companies develop product positioning strategies which are either make-to-stock, assemble-to-order, or make-to-order.

- Make-to-stock is a positioning strategy which is aimed at producing competitively-priced, standard items that can be shipped in large quantities. Manufactured materials are held in larger inventory and are widely available for replenishing retail store shelves.
- Assemble-to-order products are also made from standard components, but may be awaiting final assembly. The component parts of assemble-to-order stock can be readily assembled and delivered in short lead times and in somewhat specialized configurations.
- Make-to-order is a positioning strategy designed to take advantage of higher priced, lower volume, premium products destined for a specialized market. Companies like Dell Computer boast that they can configure a computer based on customized specifications and deliver it to the customer within an eight day lead time.

Daily Dispatch Lists

The production planners have the obligation to make sure that the right work is completed at the scheduled time so that the next manufacturing sequence can begin. When the planners and the master scheduler have agreed that the work is balanced and that there is no threat of bottleneck or overload, they must provide the data to manufacturing supervisors in the form of a "daily dispatch list." The daily dispatch list typically contains the following information:

- The dispatch list provides the items which must be completed at the work station and the expected dates of completion.
- The dispatch list shows when each operation is set to start and finish.
- The dispatch list shows pending orders, which is the work due to arrive from an earlier part of the manufacturing production sequence.
- The dispatch list establishes priorities for inbound work for shop supervisors and foremen.

The dispatch list is not set in stone, but it is the first step in getting orders assigned to assembly machine operators. After receiving the dispatch list, the work center supervisor must assign work to the operators. Oftentimes, there is variation between the planners and shop supervisors. Some of the things that must be considered while making decisions on the shop floor are:

- The priorities in sequential processing of the raw materials and components as they proceed through work stations
- The ability of the shop supervisor to recognize the limitations of operators and machinery
- The expertise of the shop supervisor and his ability to recognize which work centers can provide an advantage in set-up processes and tear-down times

POLCA

POLCA stands for "Paired-cell Overlapping Loops of Cards with Authorization."

- POLCA is a material control system.
- POLCA is a hybridized system. It combines many of the features of the old, card-based kanban technique with Materials Requirements Planning.
- POLCA was developed to be combined with Quick Response Manufacturing. The aim is to reduce lead times for all manufacturing processes.
- POLCA works best in businesses that make customized products with a variety of specifications.
- POLCA is a card-based system for controlling production. In that respect, it is similar to classic card kanban. POLCA is a method of apportioning a limited amount of work to cells, whereas kanban cards are used to pull a continuous flow of work through the cells.

POLCA systems have certain advantages over other pull systems.

- POLCA control over a shop floor means that work in progress doesn't pass downstream unless the downstream cell is available to work on it.
- Backlogged cells do not receive additional work when a POLCA system is implemented because that would add to the bottlenecked condition.
- POLCA takes advantage of variable routing paths when some downstream work stations are backlogged and others are not.
- POLCA methods are not hampered by tightly-looped work cells. POLCA cards follow a path of longer loops in a more flexible manner.
- POLCA techniques are not subject to takt time, cycle time, or other constrictions, and so may accommodate variable processes.

Product Life Cycle

The product life cycle refers to the steps required to manufacture an item. It is a stepped process, and each step in the process is tabulated and changed as the product moves along to completion.

- A general plan is provided by the master planning schedule provided by senior management.
- Material and labor estimates are matched to issue transactions attached to materials which are either on order or already ordered.
- Scheduling is of two types: operations scheduling and job scheduling. Operations scheduling is the longer-term plan that assigns start and end dates to production orders. Job scheduling breaks the process down into individual job or task segments, with specific dates and times. It also designates the work centers which will be utilized.
- When a production order is finished, the inventory module is updated with the new quantity of finished goods. In the case of WIP accounting, a journal entry is made to reduce WIP inventory.
- The production cycle ends when the actual costs of production are calculated for the amount produced.

Utilization

Utilization metrics are almost always measured in clock time. APICS defines utilization as a percentage measurement of the amount of actual time used to manufacture a product compared to the amount of time available for the activity.

- In the traditional manner of measuring equipment utilization, setup times are combined with run times and entered into the comparison as a single block of time. Certainly, there will be times when set-up and run times are isolated and measured, but utilization efficiency measurement combines the two.
- The theory of constraints adds another factor to utilization measurement, since any constraint imposes its own time limitations. For example, a shop machine might be available for 8 hours a day, but there are only enough equipment operators available to run it for 6 hours a day. In this case, measuring utilization without recognizing that constraint would result in an inaccurate and misleading measurement of utilization.

Cycle Time

APICS provides two different definitions of cycle time; the term can refer to the steps in a manufacturing activity, or it can apply to materials management.

Cycle time is a measurement of two factors:

- A production rate can be expressed in terms of blocks of time (hours being an obvious example) for the completion of a large number of mass-produced items or products.
- A production rate can be expressed in terms of the time it takes to complete a single unit of the product. For example, 60 widgets per hour would yield a single unit cycle time of 1 minute.

Cycle times have another use in addition to their use as control functions:

- Cycle times for low and high-complexity manufacturing tasks are used as a baseline for future development projects.
- Databases of cycle times can be used to generate schedules and develop reliable project timetables.

Cycle time guidelines are a way to determine whether or not a process is being improved, and to identify constraints within the process.

ORDER PROCESSING CYCLE

Each of the seven cost components of an order processing cycle has both fixed and variable costs. The seven steps, from start to completion, of an order cycle are:

- Order placement is initiated by customer contact through a variety of communication means: Internet, intranet, telephone, personal visit, etc.
- Order entry involves inputting data and communicating the information throughout the entire system. Bug-free technology systems will send data to the areas where it is needed, and not to areas where it is not.
- Credit checks are conducted on an ongoing basis to determine whether a customer has the financial standing to pay for the product.
- Documentation must accompany the purchased items. Documentation includes a clear description of material specifications, special handling instructions, and instructional or setup documentation.
- Order picking ensures that the right product(s) will be delivered to the right customer.
- Delivery must be done through reliable distribution and transportation centers.
- Invoicing and accounts receivable collection ensures that product turn-around results in gross revenues.

MAINTENANCE

Planned maintenance – a method for maintaining production equipment in which machine downtimes are scheduled for preventive maintenance and service, set either by the maintenance department and worked around by manufacturing or set by manufacturing with the cooperation of the maintenance department

Breakdown maintenance – a method, or the lack thereof, for maintaining production equipment in which the machines are operated until they malfunction, at which point the maintenance department makes necessary repairs

Accessory equipment – equipment used in manufacturing that is not associated with or dedicated to a particular work center, such as tools and gauges

Tooling – accessory equipment used for processing particular goods, usually specified in the routing, that is not typically a part of the operation performed by the work center; the same tool can be used in multiple work centers

Gauge – an accessory tool used by process personnel or inspectors to verify that the goods processed fall within specifications

Discrete ATP

ATP is the acronym for Available to Promise. APICS defines ATP as the "uncommitted portion of a company's inventory or planned production."

- Discrete ATP is derived from the Master Planning Schedule and is used to respond to customer order promising.
- Discrete ATP is just one of the three basic methods of calculating the ATP. The other two methods are variations on the same method: the cumulative without look-ahead and the cumulative with look-ahead.
- Discrete ATP is the sum of beginning inventory plus the MPS for the first period after customer commitments are subtracted up to the point where the next MPS quantity has been planned.

CPM

CPM stands for Critical Path Management. It was a technique developed by the Dupont Corporation in the 1950s. CPM is a way of managing the often large and complex activities associated with many tasks, but especially with manufacturing.

- CPM can provide a graphic view of project progression.
- CPM can be predictive of time requirements needed to complete projects.
- CPM shows the critical path of the progression of activities and functions which will result in the completion of complex processes like manufacturing.
- CPM planning involves sequencing the steps of a building or assembly process, showing their locations and proximity to each other, and delineating the critical path through the labyrinth of individual phases or work station steps that encompass the entire project.

Critical Path Management is the graphic representation of a physical trail of a work flow process. The critical path is the most efficient pathway through all of the steps in a complex process, whether it is the shutdown process of a nuclear plant or the manufacture of a consumer product. Before constructing such a critical path, it is important to obtain information about the individual process steps or tasks:

- Earliest start date at which an activity can begin. ES date assumes completion of any task preceding it.
- Earliest finish date at which a task can be completed. EF date is the time computed from ES to completion.
- Latest finish time (LF) is the latest date or time that a task can be completed without delaying the start of the next process.
- Latest start time or LS is equal to latest finish time minus the time allotted to the specific task.

EOQ

Successful manufacturing requires a smooth production flow that is flexible enough to meet varying demand. Reducing set-up times is one way of achieving this goal.

EOQ is an abbreviation for economic order quantity. EOQ originated in the belief that there is an optimum amount of inventory that can be maintained, and that it can be computed mathematically.

The EOQ model presumes that the optimum inventory can be achieved by defining a set cost of production, a demand rate, and other variables of production. The formula used to compute EOQ is:

$$EOQ = \sqrt{\frac{2SD}{PI}}$$

S = Setup costs; D = Demand rate; P = Production cost; I = Interest rate

Process Variation

It's difficult to find a manufacturing operation without a degree of process variation.

- Process variation is the certainty that, in a repetitive process like manufacturing, there will be some large or small differences in a process undertaken or in a part manufactured.
- Process variation may be so small that it is insignificant to the manufacture of a high quality product. The tolerance threshold set for manufacture is the determining criteria for successful manufacture.
- Tolerance threshold is the maximum allowable departure from a standard or specification. Beyond it, a part, process, or product cannot be used.
- An example of a process showing both process variation and threshold tolerance would be a case where a drill press operator must drill holes 1.00 inch in diameter, with a tolerance not exceeding .001 inches. Holes 1.002 inches result in rejects, as do drilled holes which are 0.998 inch.

FMEA

Failure Mode and Effect Analysis is a method of analysis often applied to the area of production management. FMEA is a method of examining an industrial process and determining where failures are most likely to occur.

- The first step of the FMEA process is to create a list of all the things that might go wrong with a process.
- FMEA then outlines the possible direct effects of a failure within each area or phase of the production process and determines its impact on other segments or phases.
- FMEA determines the cost and the impact (and its severity) of the failure on the financial outlook and profitability of the company.
- FMEA is a method of locating and isolating the potential causes of any failures that may occur.
- FMEA establishes a mathematical probability of occurrence for each potential process failure event.

FMEA assesses the ability of the supply chain system to identify a failure in its earliest stages.

Executing Plans, Implementing Physical Controls, and Reporting Results of Activities Performed

EXPEDITING AND DE-EXPEDITING

Expediting – the process of rushing materials through the manufacturing or ordering process faster than the normal lead times for the materials in order to meet rescheduled production requirements; materials being expedited have a high relative priority; expediting is also called stock chasing, and is usually overseen by a dedicated expediting department or an expediter who reports directly to the system planner.

De-expediting – the opposite of expediting; de-expediting is decreasing the relative priority of an item and slowing its manufacturing or ordering process to the regular lead-time, and sometimes includes delaying its due date; de-expediting is often overlooked in manufacturing, but enables the success of expediting to meet current priorities.

STAGING AND KITTING

Though APICS defines the two terms differently, they are different only in terms of when the materials are used:

- Staging is a way of organizing materials and components to be used in manufacturing before they are actually needed. The purpose of drawing items from inventory in a staging process is to determine if there is sufficient availability of parts and components.
- Kitting refers to the process of collecting the necessary parts and materials which are needed for production from an inventory storage bin. This kit of parts can include all of the components necessary to assemble a finished product, but the kit may, in some cases, be incomplete. The materials which are assembled in a kit must sometimes to complimented and coordinated by the placement of floor stock.

Kitting is necessary when a large number of parts are needed for a factory assembly process. It is very important that kitting not begin before the planned kit date.

- The items in a kit must be checked for mfg. order number, parent part number, and component part number. They must also be present in the necessary quantities.
- The items to be placed in the kit are derived from the picking list which, in turn, is taken from the bill of materials.
- The issue transactions are conducted as soon as the stores are picked from inventory.
- Computerized systems then match the kit issuance to the manufacturing order number, which then transmits issue transactions for each of the single items on the picking list.

Process Defects

It is inevitable that some products in a production line will contain defects as a result of mistakes made during previous steps of the production process. Many of these defective manufactured parts or products must be reworked.

- The location of the defective part is tracked, and the information sent back to management must be accurate. The production schedule cannot show process 20 (where the error occurred) if the defect was discovered in job task 40.
- If the part can be reworked, it must go back to process 20, but showing it as such will deceive the information system regarding process 30, which has already been successfully completed.
- One solution to this problem is for the shop to set up an arbitrary work station titled process 35. After process 35 (actually process 20) corrects the error, it can then be moved back to process 40, where the error was originally noted.
- The advantage of doing this, of course, is that the information system more accurately depicts the actual movement of the item.

When process errors result in defective products or parts, a manager can implement a rework order.

- Rework orders can be made on a "one-off" basis by creating a BOM with only the amount of material required to remanufacture the product or part.
- A special routing sheet is developed which entails only the limited number of work stations required to make the repair.
- A special "one-off" part number must be used until the repair has been completed and the item has been transferred to the correct part number.
- The rework order corrected in this manner will be invisible to the reporting system, however, and new orders will be issued to make up for the quantity shortfall. This is a distinct disadvantage in high volume production environments where frequent errors are likely to occur.

Reduction of Scrap

Scrap reduction should be an early factor of consideration in materials requirements planning. There are some guidelines which must be considered when considering the amount of raw material supply or components to be released to assembly.

Scrap quantity must be included in the amount of materials needed. The calculation acknowledges a specific amount of waste in the production of each single order.

Assembly of manufactured products assumes a shrinkage factor. In other words, a percentage value of any supply quantity is always scrapped during production. The amount to be released to the flow line is equal to the amount needed by the finished product plus the amount represented by the scrap percentage.

The component scrap (scrap factor) refers to the excess material used in certain parts of the manufacturing process. For example, a higher percentage of waste may occur at a single work station, while hardly any scrap is produced at other work stations.

YIELD REPORTING

Just as scrap reporting is part of materials requirements planning (MRP), so is yield reporting related to net production requirements.

- Whereas scrap reporting refers to the percentage amount of material waste incurred in the various (or single) production stages, yield reporting refers to the ratio of usable output to input.
- A production run of 10,000 widgets needed to meet a customer order will never be successful if yield reporting shows a yield factor of only 95%.
- Planners must compensate for the yield factor by increasing the manufacturing order above the stated net requirement.
- Some industries and processes are particularly prone to yield deficiencies, and so require closer monitoring than those processes which result in few errors. Continuous yield reporting under such circumstances will enhance net quantity output efficiency.

PAC

PAC is the acronym for Production Activity Control. This process is in closest contact with actual production input and output. PAC monitors and reports performance data and is a primary vehicle for corrective action. PAC may be thought of as the process of turning a company's plans into a reality.

PAC releases production orders to the manufacturing shop.

PAC assures the availability of resources, equipment, and material required for the production process.

- PAC is an input/output monitoring and corrective vehicle.
- PAC monitors WIP (work in progress) and completed orders, and reports delayed production.
- PAC establishes priority and production sequences from the daily dispatch lists and work releases.

Production Activity Control refers to the management of a wide array of activities on the manufacturing floor:

- Work scheduling must be done to provide the beginning and completion dates of individual manufacturing operations.
- Loading of work along with its proper documentation (routing documents, manufacturing specification sheets, etc.) must be completed.
- Tracking systems for work-in-progress are necessary.
- Recordation of details in accordance with the basic needs of the company and legal requirements is necessary. Data collection is necessary in the areas of worker attendance records, finished product reporting, and the details necessary for payroll computations.
- Dispatch communications systems must be in place to disseminate production data to key points in the manufacturing chain. Dispatch lists are often sent through computerized systems to which key personnel have access.
- Production metrics must be reported in the areas of efficiency, equipment utilization and functionality, and order status reports.

DATA COLLECTION

There can be a great deal of variety with respect to the type of data that must be collected in an industrial manufacturing process. The data collected depends on physical layout and the type of manufacture. The type of data collection typically required will require the display of three chief elements in nearly all cases:

- Action messages are displayed whenever upper and lower established parameters are not met. An action message may indicate that demand has shrunk and inventories are piling up. An action message may also instruct floor operators to re-schedule production runs.
- Daily dispatch lists identify work assignments before the work arrives at a work station.
- Order status reports may provide WIP data, buffer inventories, or throughput time for a specific order quantity. Order status reports may also inform the factory floor about later production or materials releases.

LOW-TECH VS. HIGH-TECH DATA COLLECTION

The complexity of data collection techniques is directly related to the complexity of operation steps. Methods of data collection can be high or low tech, depending on the facility's need for specialized and wide-ranging information. Common means of low-tech data collection include:

- Traditional manual lists consist of check sheets that require shop personnel to enter information by hand. This process can be inaccurate when transcription is required.
- Return cards can be used to follow the work around to various work centers. Entries are made (and often initialed) as each step in the process is completed. Return cards may record time, movement, or other activity.
- Job clocking relies upon the operator or laborer to record an activity.

Common means of high-tech data collection include:

- Control center operations record activity from a central point connected to work stations involved in production. This method uses machine loading boards to monitor the progress of work on each machine.
- Work station terminals are a great help in capturing real-time work processing activity. The means of capturing workflow data can involve scanners, RFID devices, keypad entry, or bar code scanners. New technologies are being developed so that work center data recording can be localized.

PRODUCTION PROGRESS REPORTING

Progress reporting on production activity may be simple or complex, depending on the number of processes and work stations utilized. The possibilities include:

- Time-elapse measurement of every operation performed on a finished product
- Checkpoint operations will measure the amount of elapsed time at various checkpoints only. It's important that these checkpoints, when chosen, be representative checkpoints that are indicative of the state of completion.
- The term order reporting refers to the recordation of only the start and end of a manufacturing order.
- Activities are tracked as they progress from count points. Count points are arbitrary in length; they may be set up to measure a process from the first work station to the last, or they may be set up to measure the amount of time elapsed from one work station to another.

- Progress reporting is a manner of determining if an order is started and completed according to schedule.
- Progress reporting may be very general and of short duration or very complex and of long duration. A manufacturing process which takes weeks to complete and requires line flows through a large number of work stations will be very detailed.
- Individual companies must determine the level of reporting detail that will best support their goals.

Delay reporting is the selective recordation of specific problem areas where delays are anticipated. Some companies place setup times in the category of delay reporting.

PUSH SYSTEMS

The push system, or centralized distribution control, is a distribution control system in which the individual distribution center managers are responsible to forecast their future demands and the planner at the central warehouse coordinates distribution requirements planning to supply the central warehouse and the individual distribution centers accordingly. Advantages of the push system include the overall and future planning aspects rather than the reaction to individual demands prevalent in the pull system, the resulting ability to coordinate manufacturing with the distribution demand, the transferability of stock between distribution centers as appropriate due to centralized planning, and the ease of implementation of new policies. Disadvantages of the push system include higher communication costs and the physical separation between what is actually happening at individual distribution centers and the decision making affecting those distribution centers.

PULL SYSTEMS

Traditional push systems, wherein the top hierarchy released materials for manufacturing without regard for flow line demand, created bottlenecks, which reduced overall efficiency and profits.

- The pull system focuses on demand; demand dictates the amount of material pulled from stores, inventory, or even from suppliers.
- Pull system phenomena occur at all levels of the supply and production chain.
- Replenishment cycles at retail stores can send demand data to central distribution locations.
- Diminution of supply at distribution center locations sends demand data to factory production sites.
- Factory flow lines send demand data upstream to in-house stores, which maintain lean inventories of materials and components needed for manufacturing.
- In-house stores send demand data to suppliers and vendors.

The key factor to remember is that demand pulls the supply from upstream at a level and pace needed to sustain a continuous flow of finished products to the consumer. It does so without unnecessary inventory build-up or bottlenecks.

KANBAN

Kanban is a concept derived from the early days of Japanese auto manufacturing. A system of flash cards was used to signal demand to upstream suppliers. Although modern kanban may be computerized, the concept is still used as a method of achieving lean and agile production efficiencies.

- Kanban reduces the number of unnecessary components moving through the manufacturing cycles, which prevents bottlenecks.
- When excess supply is removed from the manufacturing cycle through kanban, the root problems which might cause delays in production can more readily be seen and addressed.
- Kanban is a pull system. This means that the system pulls materials from upstream suppliers as the supplies are needed.
- The ideal kanban state is to have an economic order quantity of one. This means that the ideal condition in kanban is to have one unit of inventory for each unit of product currently being assembled.
- Kanban techniques can employ traditional methods other than the use of flash cards. Kanban can employ empty containers, tags, or other signs that additional supplies are needed in specific quantities.

Kanban is a tried and true method of increasing manufacturing efficiency. The gain in production efficiencies resulting from the Japanese implementation of kanban in the auto industry has resulted in the technique being applied in most modern manufacturing facilities. It is clear that kanban can increase company profits.

- Kanban reduces production costs since EOQ (economic order quantity) is improved by matching inventories to the quantities needed.
- Reducing EOQ as close as possible to the ideal point of one has the result of reducing set-up costs, inventory carrying costs, and, ultimately, the total costs of production.
- When inventories are reduced to the quantities needed for current production levels, underlying manufacturing problems are revealed and can be remedied. This further streamlining of the assembly manufacturing process leads to greater efficiency and increased profits for the manufacturer.

Kanban is a technique adopted to prevent bottlenecks by matching the amount of inventory to the quantities needed to meet production demand.

The ideal kanban state is to have an economic order quantity of one. This means that the ideal condition in kanban is to have one unit of inventory for each unit of product currently being assembled.

Initial kanban techniques employed the use of cards to inform upstream suppliers of the need for parts or components.

Adaptive kanban techniques which accomplish the same purpose make use of computers.

Kanban techniques can employ traditional methods other than the use of flash cards. Kanban can employ empty containers, tags, or other signs that additional supplies are needed in specific quantities.

Kanban Square and Single Card Kanban

Kanban is a concept that was first used in the early days of Japanese auto manufacturing to signal increased demand to upstream suppliers. It is an inexpensive method of controlling excessive and costly inventories and preventing bottlenecking in work centers.

- The kanban square is simply a square painted on the factory floor. Material needed for a manufacturing process is placed in the square for use in the work center. When the square is empty, the empty kanban square is the signal for replenishment of the part or component.
- Single card kanban can involve using the traditional cards that were used by early Japanese auto manufacturers, but it may also involve the use of tags or colored items that call attention to the need for replenishment of supply. It can employ bins or containers as well. A worker presenting an empty bin serves as the signal for replenishment of supply.

Transaction Costing

Transaction costing is a method of accounting for those costs which do not add value to a product. Transaction costing includes such activities as documentation, ordering from suppliers, inspecting incoming raw materials, components, or subassemblies.

- Vendor scheduling is a way of reducing transactional costs of purchase orders.
- Delivery of materials to the location where they will be utilized rather than to shipping and receiving areas will reduce transaction costs.
- Kanban saves on the documentation or data input steps required for scheduling and individual work order instructions.
- Backflushing and the use of floor stock reduce material handling and the documentation steps resulting from material issued or retrieved from inventory areas.

ABC

Traditional accounting cost categories include elements such as salaries, wages, depreciation, rent/phone/utilities, maintenance, and energy. Very often, this type of traditional accounting has failed to recognize hidden costs.

ABC, or activity based costing, is changing the costing philosophy by shifting the point of control from standard categories like those noted above. Instead, resources are allocated to those areas that are deemed to be most important.

The type of category that can drive the process of activity based costing could be an activity like order picking. ABC accounting of order picking might include the number of product order lines to be moved, making it a less static category than it would be if traditional accounting methods were used.

ABC is a way of matching a company's resources to the activities it must perform.

- ABC differs from conventional methods of allocating money to individual department categories like wages, depreciation, rent/phone/utilities, maintenance, and fuel.
- Merely deciding to spend more money on a single budget allocation item like "maintenance" won't help the bottom line if the problem is being caused by poor management of broad-based cleanup activities.

- Activity based costing is achieved by looking for the forces and folds within the manufacturing process that drive costs higher. It also seeks those elements of the process which enhance profits and which can be made more efficient by the application of additional resources to processes defined by specific activities.
- Activity based costing often involves the practice of averaging data in the interest of identifying activities which either consume resources unnecessarily or enhance profits.

While ABC is still an allocated cost method of assessment, it relies more on customer service analysis for profitability and cost savings.

Traditional accounting cost categories include: wages, depreciation, rent/phone/utilities, maintenance, and fuel.

Activity based costing may have the following accounting categories. The types of factors which drive the process are identified:

- Sales order processing may be based on the number of orders.
- Holding inventory costs may include storage, deterioration, finance costs, and materials handling.
- Picking categories are concerned with packaging and the number of product order lines to be moved in single units or family groups.
- Loading costs are compiled based on weights and volumes.
- Transportation and delivery costs are affected by the location of the customer and their distance from the inventory center.
- Problem solving costs are those associated with returns, problems with customers, etc.

Activity based costing steps required to bring a batch of products to market may include:

- Day One: Purchase and receive $60,000 worth of raw material and components.
- Day Two: Issue half the materials to the factory floor at a cost of $30,000.
- Day Three: Apply labor cost to the materials at a cost of $5,000.
- Day Four: Recognize depreciation costs of $50,000 for the month.
- Day Five: Apply a variable overhead cost of $5,000.
- Day Six: Transfer 5,000 finished mathematics calculators from WIP to finished goods inventory.
- Day Seven: Ship half of the 5,000 finished goods items to retail customers.
- Note that days need not be sequential, which will allow for other scheduled manufactured products. Be aware that activity based costing uses active verbs like ship, transfer, apply, recognize, apply, or issue.

The purposes of ABC financial accounting are to improve planning, cost estimating, and decision support.

- ABC systems assign logic to cost assignment and identify cost drivers.
- Customer demand is an example of a cost driver.
- ABC systems are activity based. The categories used in ABC systems employ active verbs in activity classifications, such as "process national invoices."
- The cost drivers are attributed to different segments, including customers, products, suppliers, and other segments which stimulate production.

- The diversity of activity which drives costs can be evaluated more closely and the evaluation can be based on the nature of the activity.
- ABC allows "tagging" of the activities so that different levels of activity can be graded according to the level at which they drive costs.

BOM FILE

The Bill of Materials file contains vital information necessary to support the planning modules.

- Bill of Material information is essential in ordering re-supply and replacement parts. The Bill of Materials (BOM) file reveals specific information regarding the parts used to manufacture a finished product.
- A BOM may be "single layer" and consist of one component part, or it may be a multi-layered configuration of components. BOM information, however, is always fed into the planning system as a single-layer piece of information. The computer software will automatically link the parent level to sub-assemblies.
- It is important to note that assembly part numbers are sequenced alphabetically, while raw materials and single parts are sequenced numerically.

VISIBILITY

Visual controls are a key concept in JIT manufacturing. Invisibility causes confusion and an ensuing lack of direction.

- Visibility of overall activity is a key component of communicating production goals to all individuals involved in production planning and processes. Shop floor managers can implement visibility measures such as:
- Posting of the daily schedule showing current and anticipated production levels, downtime, and output reports
- The use of visual indicators and gauges to monitor potential equipment problems
- Posting of individual work center figures such as production and reject levels
- Inventory measurement showing WIP and buffer inventory
- Visibility should be implemented in tool locations, with space provided to account for and match each tool.

INVENTORY TRANSACTION PROCESS

A basic inventory transaction process should be in place before inventory moves from storage, to manufacture, and finally to the customer. The steps in setting up a system for routing of inventory transactions are:

- Construct an inventory transaction flow map which shows all work centers, materials storage locations, required documentation points, transaction types, and account numbers.
- Spread flow time information throughout the work place so that people are aware of successes and deficiencies in moving material through the plant.
- Set cutoff times for posting data requiring transaction accounting.
- Just as materials may go into kanban squares or boxes, so should the locations where documentation is required be clearly marked.

Key transactions are shipping, receiving, and batch controls. These must be logged and continuously reviewed for errors. Logging can be very helpful in reconstruction after system crashes.

FOUR-WALL INVENTORY MANAGEMENT

A four-wall inventory system is one that makes no location distinctions within the manufacturing facility. Three key practices in managing this type of inventory are identified below.

- ABC cycle counting requires that a portion of the storage inventory be counted in a time period-driven cycle. One percent of items or locations may be counted each day, with a full cycle completed every 100 days. This eliminates the disruption inherent in physical inventory counting.
- Container and location tracking employs scanners or RFID devices to physically track barcoded pallets, bins, railcars, or other staging areas.
- Real-time warehouse management systems support container and location tracking.

BACKFLUSHING

Backflushing is a manufacturing process which can enhance synchronous manufacturing.

- Backflushing is a means of obtaining materials needed for manufacture and deducting amounts from the Bill of Materials.
- The standard way of delivering raw products or components to the assembly line is to obtain the components or parts from storage inventory during the pre-production or readying phases of manufacture.
- Backflushing is a post-production process; it is implemented after regular assembly manufacturing is well under way. It is a production control mechanism that results in greater efficiency and less wasted effort.
- Backflushing is a much easier way of keeping production system counts when the number of supply order items received and completed is more than the finished product count.

RFID

RFID or Radio Frequency Identification is the latest technology used to track the movement of vehicles, people, and materials. A key advantage is that it traces movement in real time, rather than at specific counting points, such as the shipping or receiving area of a manufacturing firm.

- RFID is comparatively expensive technology. The high cost of an initial investment in RFID must be balanced against the benefits obtained. How important is the accuracy associated with RFID to your operation?
- The true costs of an RFID installation? RFID wafers or chips can currently be programmed with varying amounts of data. The more specialized the data, the more expensive the wafer. Consider the cost of RFID readers or translators.
- Technical analysis is necessary to determine whether there is significant interference risk from other radio frequencies used in a particular environment.
- Will real-time tracking help the bottom line? RFID is clearly useful in tracking military materials or medicines, but is it helpful to a manufacturer of ball bearings?

The least expensive way of tracking products moving from supplier to manufacturer to retail customer is through the extensive use of bar-coding, barcode scanners, and SKU (stock-keeping unit codes). As the price of RFID or Radio Frequency Identification technology continues to decrease, more facilities will probably adopt the technology. RFID will likely soon be viewed as the most efficient and accurate means of tracking products and measuring cycle times.

- Barcodes identify the product at counting points. They do not provide a continuous record of movement. RFID tags identify the product, provide its current or past locations, determine the expiration date of the product, and provide any other information that has been programmed into the RFID chip.
- RFID makes huge amounts of data available for analysis. This information can be quickly shared to produce a system of manufacture and distribution which operates closer to "real-time" than ever before.
- RFID tags can be read by electronic readers. The information is then transmitted through a sensor network that joins supply chain components together.

Barring technical difficulties which may be infrequently encountered, RFID provides near total visibility in the supply chain. As such, it is an ideal tool of analysis and remediation for manufacturing bottlenecks.

- Internal and external supply chains can be tracked with lower-cost RFID tags. Irregularities in materials flow can be identified in the interest of leaning the materials flow process.
- RFID data transmitted to a central control operation system can trigger replenishment and assist in rerouting defective product output.
- RFID can measure movement at any point in the internal or external supply chain, as opposed to traditional methods which provide data at select checkpoints.
- Programmed RFID tags can track material flow in such a way as to react with plus or minus deviation settings to trigger a variety of corrective actions.

Bar Coding

Bar coding is the process of placing stickers or labels that can be read by scanners or other optical reading systems on retail products. Bar coding is used in lieu of pricing labels because it has distinct advantages.

- The scanner used to read the bar code can be linked to a price database in order to keep abreast of price increases and/or discounts.
- The bar code system can also be used to track on-shelf inventory and set replenishment cycles in motion.
- Bar coding reduces labor costs because little time has to be devoted to the application of pricing labels on single products. The customer can see the price by looking at the shelf rack where the item is stocked.
- Bar coding eliminates keying errors by check-out personnel.

Bar coding is one of the least expensive methods of automating the tracking of materials used in manufacturing. Bar coding is far less expensive than old-fashioned and work-intensive manual checking or new, high-tech methods like RFID.

- Bar coding is used in manufacturing to monitor the flow of parts and materials in flow lines. In some cases, VDU or reader devices are placed along conveyor belts and positioned so that they will read the data written into the bar code.

- The use of bar coding in manufacturing eliminates keying errors or other inaccuracies associated with repetitive mechanized activity.
- Bar coding can also trigger the replenishment cycles and signal when additional materials must be moved from stores or inventory.

Code 39 is a form of bar coding often used for larger, bulk items in the auto and defense industries, as well as in other manufacturing environments.

- Code 39 is an alpha-numeric method which can be read with a barcode scanner. Most barcode scanners have Code 39 set as their default read capability.
- A disadvantage of Code 39 is that it requires a larger label since its characters occupy more space than what is required in other coding concepts (Code 128, for example). This characteristic of Code 39 makes it inconvenient to use in facilities that manufacture smaller products.
- Code 39 bar coding can be easily recognized because of its code referencing characteristics. Code 39 is derived from the fact that 3 of the 9 bars that constitute a codeword are wide bars, while the remaining ones are narrow.

CAD

The simultaneous transmission of information from end to end in the production-assembly chain provides unprecedented synchronicity and visibility to the process. Technologies have also greatly expanded design and engineering capabilities.

- CAD/CAM or Computer Assisted Design allows for flexible manufacturing, meaning profit can be made with smaller batch sizes.
- The time between design, production, and sales is vastly diminished by Computer Assisted Design. However, this sort of streamlined design requires a higher degree of visibility. It also means that a number of assembly phases must be synchronized.
- Production can be further synchronized to demand because of the speed at which information can flow.
- Intranets can serve as powerful cross-departmental tools for horizontal and vertical communication within an organization.
- Intranet increases workforce productivity by helping users locate and view information relevant to their tasks.

Transportation Logistics

Transportation decisions are not made in a vacuum. The complexity of these choices means they have implications beyond the initial decision, and will impact the bottom line of profitability in sometimes unforeseen ways.

- A decision to ship to a central distribution center will save money in the first step of product distribution because most freight goes to the same central distribution location. Beyond the distribution warehouse, costs may be minimized or they may increase, depending on a variety of factors.
- Having a centralized distribution warehouse will require increased coordination with end-user customers and perhaps an additional investment in communications technology. A positive outcome of this action might be that products will be located close to customer regional areas.

- Centralized warehousing requires additional storage, spoilage, pilferage, financing, and material handling costs. These costs must be evaluated against the cost advantages gained by being closer to regional markets.

Traditional transportation categories developed during the era of increased regulation. The current trend has been toward decreased federal and state regulation of the shipping industries. Some critics point out that it is now possible to ship "air freight shipments that never see an airplane."

- Traditional categories are described as long-haul, truckload, less-than-truckload, air freight, rail, and waterways. Very often, a shipment will travel on a combination of these.
- Modern transportation thinking breaks categories down into standard hub-system services and individualized door-to-door service. Each of these has different pricing structures; truckload services generally charge by the mile. LTL (less-than-truckload) services base their prices on volume and weight.
- Speed, service, cost, reliability, and security of operations are primary considerations when making transportation decisions.

Inventory Storage

Efficient storage is a key component in keeping manufacturing costs down. An efficient storage strategy must be custom-tailored to fit the kind of operation it supports.

- Point of use storage locates unused stock adjacent to the work center(s) where it will be used. This is effective in assembly line operations but, unless combined with back flushing, can result in a loss of control over the production process.
- Point of manufacture storage is located closer to flow lines than point of use storage.
- Limited access storage is a formal method of controlling what goes in and what comes out of inventory. The method lends itself to kitting. It is a higher cost method, but is necessary for high-value stock.

The three chief methods of inventory storage used in limited access inventory locations are dedicated, random, and zone storage.

- Dedicated storage is of a type wherein each part has a permanent location. The volume of space is sufficient to accommodate whatever inventory is needed to sustain production.
- Random storage requires an efficient monitoring system because materials movers tend to access the materials more easily. The use of stock in random storage must be supervised so that it is properly sequenced into the production process.
- Zone storage is a method of storage which combines dedicated and random storage. Inventory is divided into zones, with random storage implemented into each zone.

A large, high-volume manufacturing firm with several facilities devoted to production will certainly require automation in a warehouse management system.

- Inventory storage planners should consider the type of handling equipment which is available for use. Can handling equipment retrieve items with different SKUs if they are combined?
- What bar coding or RFID technologies can be paid for, implemented, and utilized?
- Can the system accommodate supplier parts or package labeling constraints?
- Does the inventory storage system allow for efficient pick batch functionality? What picking methods are supported?
- Is there a methodology established for hazardous materials handling?

Materials Handling

Internal materials handling can be facilitated by adhering to a set of common rules:

- Lessen the distance between operations so that the item being manufactured can move from one work station to another without 3rd party handling.
- Sort or kit materials accurately before they begin movement along downstream routing circuits to diminish expensive alternative routing of reject material.
- Employ the techniques of back flushing, point of use storage, and floor stock to minimize activity at expensive limited access storage areas.
- Overlap operations so as to limit inventory buildup.
- Integrate the external supply chain to be synchronous with flow line production rates. The use of technology allows sharing of production rate information with vendors, and should assist in assuring steady delivery rates.

Procurement

Procurement is the acquisition of materials and/or components needed for product manufacturing. The method of procurement must be matched to the type of production in a specific facility. Planning is the first step in matching the procurement methods to the manufacturing outlook.

- Lot-based procurement means that the purchasing agent has obtained price quotes for a particular lot size from a host of potential suppliers.
- The procurer then makes the decision based on price, quality, and on how certain he is that delivery will be made on the date the materials are needed.
- Lot-based procurement means that there is no ongoing commitment to the supplier after the purchase order contract is completed and the materials are delivered to specification.

Procurement supply scheduling is one method used to acquire materials and/or components needed for product manufacturing. This method of procurement lends itself to some types of manufacturing.

- Companies with an ongoing need for materials or components for manufacturing may choose to procure them through the process of scheduling suppliers.
- The terms of scheduled deliveries are spelled out in the delivery contract. The total volume of material to be delivered under contract may be specified on a yearly basis, or the contract may be open-ended, meaning the volume of goods to be delivered is specified in the contract based on the manufacturer's production schedule.
- Prices are specified for the length of the contract, and cannot be re-negotiated until the contract expiration date.
- The supplier is responsible for balancing the flow of materials to match the manufacturer's demand when this method of scheduling suppliers is used.

The release system of procurement is a method of procurement which allows a degree of long-term flexibility while still meeting specific short-term production needs.

- The release system of procurement allows for better planning by a supplier who may have to meet the material demands of several different companies.
- The release system of procurement projects a manufacturing facility's long-term needs and transmits this data to the supplier.

- The same facility makes a concrete and specific short-term order for supplies and provides a specific delivery date. The short-term releases are issued on a periodic basis, either weekly, monthly, quarterly, or whatever short term time frame is necessary for continuous manufacturing.

The procurement process requires advance planning activity by the manufacturing facility. Procurement is especially difficult when new suppliers must be sought as the result of new ventures.

- The first step in procurement is information gathering. Research must be done to assess the availability and capabilities of potential suppliers.
- After a list of appropriate potential suppliers has been made, the manufacturer will submit requests for a proposal to deliver materials, along with a price quotation.
- Background research is then conducted to review the credentials of the prospective supplier.
- Contract negotiation begins after a supplier has been chosen. Price, availability, and the customization requirements are set before the contract is authorized.
- Fulfillment of the contract is completed and payment is made.
- If the manufacturing firm is happy with the product supplier's performance, this may lead to a renewal contract. Quality and reliability of the supplier are continuously evaluated with a view toward future needs.

Goals of the Modern Manufacturing Process

The modern streamlined manufacturing process may have a variety of short-term goals, but the master planning schedulers must adhere to the long-term goals of improving operating efficiency, maintaining minimum inventory, and improving customer service.

- Improving operating efficiency involves taking a holistic approach to production. This represents a departure from traditional methods, in which each work station would manage efficiencies as if it were an independent entity. The typical traditional methods gave one operational segment an advantage at the expense of others.
- Maintaining minimum inventory can save carrying costs, which are estimated to represent between 30 to 35 percent of total productivity costs. This is a high price to pay merely to have inventory occupying physical space and incurring debt.
- Customer service objectives must be streamlined to deliver the right products at the right time. This means properly identifying customer markets and providing the level of service that will guarantee maximum profits.

Planning and Operational Levels of Manufacturing

The interface between the planning and operational levels of a manufacturing system requires an efficient information flow. The interfaces between the planning of top management, operations planning, and operations execution must support the channeling of vital information along a multi-path circuit.

- Input from top management planners must interface with plant manufacturing and execution in order to maintain valid production schedules and operating priorities.
- Synchronizing the manufacturing process can be accomplished through the interface of different management levels. Technology and communications interfaces can efficiently share vital data throughout the manufacturing enterprise.
- Interfaces between operational levels of factory production will reduce cycle-times, set-up times, and product lead times.

Make-to-Order and Make-to-Stock Companies

Manufacturing policies are established in advance by the master planners. Two common types of operations are make-to-order and make-to-stock.

- Make-to-order companies are willing to accommodate the customer's design and quality expectations.
- Make-to-order companies generally rely on demand forecasting to determine production levels. Once the types of items required for manufacture is determined, the make-to-order company will maintain connections to the suppliers of raw materials and component parts. In this way, the lead time to the customer is shortened.
- Make-to-stock companies manufacture consumer goods for which demand is generally stable. The demand for items like soap, cleansers, or toothpaste, for example, is fairly stable. Large fluctuations in demand for these types of goods are rarely observed.
- Make-to-order manufacturing orders materials from its suppliers in accordance with sales estimates and historical research data.
- Make-to-order manufacturing may respond to warehouse replenishment orders or may employ a DRP (distribution requirements planning) strategy.

Production Process Designs

Production process design consists of three traditional elements which are useful in describing the production environment: flow shop production, job shop production, and fixed site production.

- Flow shop production has a product flow scheme which does not change in sequence. Flow shop production can utilize a continuous flow system or a combination of continuous and intermittent flow systems. The type of flow process selected is determined by the type of product produced. Liquid natural gas and petroleum are readily adaptable to the continuous flow process, as the raw materials are developed into a variety of products.
- Job shops are organized on the basis of function. Work moves from one work center to another based on the type of work necessary to produce a finished product.
- Fixed site production models are those in which materials, labor, and equipment are brought to a fixed location. Fixed site production is used in shipbuilding enterprises or in the manufacture of large objects like giant cargo aircraft.

MRP

The Materials Requirements Planner (MRP) has the task of maintaining balance in the manufacturing operation. Supply and demand must be monitored with a view to correcting imbalances and bottlenecks.

- MRP logic is based on basic assumptions, which may vary somewhat from real-world conditions. MRP logic assumes that capacity is unlimited and that scheduled production start and end dates remain constant.
- When CRP data shows that the production system in a work center is overloaded, corrective action is necessary. The first area to consider during the process of resolving system overloading is the Production Activity Control (PAC).

An effective strategy to resolve bottlenecks and overloads would be to revise the order dates. The Materials Requirements Planner should work closely with the Master Scheduler to determine how these alterations would impact final assembly and shipment to the customer.

A Materials Requirements Planning approach to manufacturing has advantages and disadvantages. These weaknesses and strengths must be considered when determining what kind of approach is best for the manufacturing process.

Advantages:

- Materials requirements planning results in lower inventory levels.
- The increased visibility of material flow and production allows for better management of components.
- MRP has been shown to have resulted in few stockouts.
- MRP has the distinct advantage of coordinating with the MPS (master planning schedule).
- MRP operations typically have fewer production disruptions.

Disadvantages:

- MRP does not address the issue of lot size.
- MRP relies on the fall-back safety of slack time rather than safety stock.
- MRP relies on assumptions such as constant, known lead times.
- MRP requires a tremendous amount of data and effort to set up. In the set-up process, there is a tendency to inflate initial values in order to avoid start-up issues.

Lean Manufacturing

Leanness in productive capacity is not the same as Just-In-Time manufacturing, but the two concepts have many elements in common.

- Lean manufacturing means that supply inventories are matched to production capabilities and speed, and are not allowed to build up to excess.
- Lean manufacturing requires speedy communication and transparency throughout the supply line. It involves teamwork between departments rather than competition.
- Lean manufacturing makes efficient use of resources and economies of scale.
- Lean manufacturing makes use of common components.

- Lean manufacturing often postpones final processing or finishing until customer demand is significantly more predictable.
- Lean manufacturing strives to reduce supplier lead times through more stable and reliable relationships.

Lean manufacturing can be best analyzed and measured when the relationships between different factors are understood.

- Run time is the amount of time consumed to complete a single operation on a part or component. Run times are compressed or expanded according to the efficiencies of the operating function. The run times for simple activities like drilling or stamping operations can be decreased or increased by many factors: reliability of equipment, MTBF (mean time between failures), staffing or labor issues, and other factors.
- Reducing run times means that the capacity requirement is also reduced. Reducing the run time for one process means that time is available for another activity. A lot consisting of 100 items will consume less manufacturing capacity, making the assembly plant capable of handling more production.
- Lot size is the standard amount of product processed in a "batch," which refers to products produced within the same production run. Smaller batches will reduce run times and shrink the capacity requirements, but will also result in more set-up time.

Knowing what to do on the factory floor is the direct result of a policy foundation geared toward lean rather than traditional manufacturing methods.

- Managerial staff and managers must be broadly trained, rather than specialized.
- No amount of rejects or variance in quality should be accepted. The goal is zero defects.
- Communication should take place informally and horizontally, rather than through hierarchies. Communication flows as much from the bottom among line workers as it does through traditional hierarchies.
- Equipment should be mobile, standardized, general purpose, and flexible.
- Production should be organized into cells, rather than into specialized stages grouped by process.
- Continuous processes are preferable to batch processes. Production systems must operate with as little work-in-process inventory as possible.
- Excess inventory and defective end products represent wasted efficiency.

Lean manufacturing depends upon the smooth flow of materials throughout the production process. The movement of large machines through the shop floor often constitutes an unnecessary obstacle to efficient manufacturing. The tendency toward small batch sizes has led to more efficient production because:

- Small, light containers of standard size are more visible in terms of quantity and purpose. These can be moved from one work station to the next without forklifts or cranes.
- Tote boxes are standardized containers which make accounting for parts easier because they are configured with separators. Visible amounts of materials means that work in progress can be more accurately controlled.
- Reusable containers should be the rule, and will cut down on the amount of waste which must be stored, moved, and disposed of. Reusable containers are at the heart of the kanban system of parts replenishment on the flow line.

Data reporting is a tool that guides the way to lean manufacturing. Inventory management is a vital part of any manufacturing system, and refers to both incoming and outgoing inventory. Inventory managers must measure inventory in many different forms.

Finished goods inventory must be constantly monitored and maintained at levels that are consistent with demand. Finished goods inventory is also termed cycle stock.

Raw material, parts, and component inventories must be measured and maintained according to drumbeat level.

Work in progress inventory is a frequently missed or inaccurately accounted for inventory quantity. Complicating this type of inventory is its movement downstream, variable lead times in each phase of production, and variable volumes at peak times.

Customer satisfaction depends on providing a quality finished product to the customer at the right time. Lean manufacturing accomplishes that goal by shrinking queue times, throughput times, and order cycle times.

- The order cycle time represents the elapsed time from order to delivery. Order cycle times should be worked and reworked toward maximum efficiency.
- Throughput time can refer to the time spent in and out of inventory. It is also used and measured as a ratio of the number of items manufactured within an hour of scheduled production. Sixty widgets manufactured in one hour would mean a throughput time of one widget per minute.

Queue time represents the amount of time inventory spends waiting in line before it proceeds to the next manufacturing step or is routed to the next work station. An excessive number of items in queue or queue times that are excessively long require action to prevent bottlenecking of the system.

The concept of lean manufacturing was developed by Japanese automobile manufacturers in the 1970s. In order to compete with the Big Three auto makers and the wide variety of choices offered by GM, Ford, and Chrysler, the Japanese auto industry responded with an auto industry which produced less in terms of choice and more in terms of value and price.

This leanness in the manufacturing process was attained by:

- Focusing on economies of scale and the efficient management of resources. Elimination of waste, shrinking of inventory, and kanban created visibility in the manufacturing process.
- Common components were used, and this had the effect of making supply more reliable and consistent. Flow lines were less likely to experience bottleneck conditions, and when they did, remedies were soon applied.
- Supplier response time was decreased through better relationships and continuous communication with a smaller number of suppliers.
- Standard products and predictable demand forecasting were combined to produce company profits. Auto platforms were similar. Components were reliable. High standards of quality were continuously sought.

Moving Equipment

Small moving equipment is often used to maneuver factory materials in tight spaces.

- Two-wheeled hand trolleys, sometimes termed "hand trucks," are designed for use in narrow passageways. Material containers may be stacked on top of each other. The strength of the frame and the worker are key factors in determining the weight and the size of the loads that can be safely moved.
- Four-wheeled trolleys are easier to handle for moving parts, and may be available in sizes suitable for applications for which they will be used. The advantage of these is that they can be equipped with sides to accommodate certain types of material.
- Two and four-wheeled trolleys cannot handle pallets of material. These can be moved through the use of hand pallet trucks, which have a typical capacity of one ton. Hand pallet trucks are equipped with hydraulic jacks, which raise heavy materials from the shop floor.
- Motorized hand pallet trucks are typically equipped with electrical motors to aid in moving heavier loads in spaces where forklifts cannot be used.

Forklifts and reach trucks are commonly used in factories and warehouses to move materials too heavy to be moved by smaller equipment.

- Lift trucks are manufactured to design specifications, which must be observed for safe handling. One hundred deaths per year are caused by forklift accidents; most of them are caused by tipping and loads exceeding counterbalance capacities.
- Forklift specifications warn that maximum rated loads must never be exceeded, and that tires, hydraulic controls, and hydraulic lines must be inspected before use.
- Forklifts may be powered by battery, liquefied gas, or by gasoline or diesel engine.
- Reach trucks are an electric variation of the forklift. They differ in that they have tighter turning circles and do not carry their loads in front of the vehicle body.

Materials Suppliers

With quality as the goal, APICS has reinforced the close relationship between materials suppliers and the manufacturing firm.

- APICS certification provides assurance that a supplier will provide high quality components and materials to the manufacturing firm. APICS sets standards for supplier firms that may be related to cost, delivery time, safety, environment, and ISO.
- Certification by APICS means that a supplier can meet specific schedule requirements and can deliver components and materials directly to the place where they are to be used.
- APICS certification means that parts can go directly to the flow line in the interest of lean manufacturing. Delivering incoming material(s) directly to the assembly line eliminates handling and inspection in the receiving area.
- APICS certified direct delivery eliminates costly inventory storage and carry costs, and saves time in throughput.

ISO 9000 is a set of international standards to which suppliers must adhere in order to be registered to supply materials and components in Europe, the Pacific Rim, and the Americas.

- ISO 9000 identifies international standards used to document quality specifications for global trade.
- The standards are generalized and not limited to specific industries or services.
- ISO 9000 standards were developed by the ISO, or International Standards Organization.

- Currently, the International Standards Organization (ISO) is staffed with personnel from over 100 countries.
- Originally conceived as a set of manufacturing standards with military origins, it currently entails a book of procedures directed at all products and services in all business segments.
- The most recent version of ISO 9000 standards takes a process approach, with a customer focus on continuous improvement. Older ISO standards were restricted to product and service specifications.

ISO 9000 certification is a mandatory requirement of doing business in European countries. General steps that a firm wishing to be registered and certified must take include:

- Create a steering committee comprised of progressive management personnel.
- Management personnel must work together to create a project plan for ISO 9000 certification.
- Analyze the processes of quality standardization to identify where the processes being used to provide quality conflict with ISO 9000 processes and standards.
- Management personnel must enlist engineers and floor experts to write policies for system procedures and to develop manuals of product quality specifications.
- Employees must be trained in new procedures and materials requirements. Training records and other records dating back at least three months must be available for examination.
- Manufacturing facilities must be swept clear of uncontrolled documents and equipment that do not meet calibration specifications.
- A visit by an ISO 9000 registrar can certify compliance and make recommendations.

The International Organization for Standards (ISO) quality system (ISO 9000) is a set of procedures which will guide a manufacturer toward the production and delivery of consistently high quality products. The framework of ISO 9000 includes all aspects of the product value chain, from management philosophy to continuous process improvement.

The individual areas of ISO 9000 compliance are as follows:

- Management responsibility/Inspection and testing
- Quality system/Control of inspection and metrics
- Contract management /Inspection and testing
- Design control/Control of non-conforming product
- Document and data control/Test equipment
- Purchasing/Materials handling
- Corrective and preventive action storage
- Packaging/Control of customer-supplier product
- Preservation and delivery
- Product identification and traceability
- Control of quality records
- Process control
- Training

The trend in lean manufacturing is to streamline the supply chain by developing better relationships with a smaller number of suppliers. This trend points the way toward a certification process, in which manufacturers follow certification steps in approving organizations that supply products, parts, and components for their assembly processes.

- Obtaining the lowest cost of supply is not the sole objective in certifying a supplier. Delivery capacity, quality, and the amount of expense required for warehousing, repackaging, and reworking are also factors to consider.
- Making unrealistic demands with regard to delivery or quality is not a fair way to assess a supplier's capability. Criteria of certification must be realistic. Realistic goals are those which the manufacturing company can itself deliver to its own customers.

When a firm tries to increase quality by assessing the merits of individual suppliers, it sends an audit team to investigate and discuss options for service delivery and quality improvement.

- Audit and evaluation teams must gauge the attitude of the supplier towards achieving the revised supplier quality standards. Can the supplier work cooperatively to develop and improve new products?
- Audit and evaluation teams must determine if the supplier keeps careful records of service levels, delivery times, customer satisfaction, and quality product design.
- Audit teams determine whether TQI, DRIFT, or similar process efficiency improvement techniques are used by the supplier.
- Audit teams determine whether JIT delivery can be continuously maintained in the long term. A suitable location would help in achieving this objective.
- Audit teams must determine whether the supplier has the productive capacity to meet volume and quality demands.

Nowhere is the impact of international quality requirements felt as severely as it is in the US automobile industry. A globally competitive environment is not a forgiving one when it comes to parts and component quality for automotive suppliers.

- The automotive Big Three have adapted standards of ISO – 9000 to their industry, calling it QS – 9000.
- Current quality assurance practices of the suppliers of automotive components and automobile sub-assemblers are audited every six months by their registrars as a condition of maintaining the supplier registration integrity.
- Seventy percent of all Tier I suppliers are QS – 9000 certified.
- Other suppliers anticipate completing the registration process for QS-900 certification within three to five years.

Inspecting 100% of incoming and outgoing materials has become common practice among suppliers who deliver to the US auto industry Big Three.

The trend in modern companies is to shrink the number of suppliers and obtain better quality raw materials and components. A smaller number of suppliers means swift communication of mutual objectives as well as a more flexible and responsive supplier system.

The quality expected from suppliers is not limited to product or component specifications. Quality is aimed at customer satisfaction, and encompasses aesthetics, design, packaging, durability, and delivery.

Modern manufacturing relies on strategic partnerships with suppliers. An up-to-date and very recent example of supplier relationships concerns the suppliers of screen glass for LCD televisions.

A single supplier now produces all the LCD screens for three major LCD television producers: Sharp, Sony, and Samsung.

Successful manufacturing is quality manufacturing, and depends heavily on materials control. The emphasis must be on preventing defective materials from being delivered to the factory.

Quality materials must also be consistently delivered in a timely and reliable manner.

- Timely delivery is accomplished by a high degree of pipeline visibility. Manufacturers must be able to see the supplier activity that affects them. Suppliers must have pipeline visibility into manufacturing demand, which will allow them to forecast reliable delivery, which supports lean inventories. Intranet and extranet are primary means of accomplishing pipeline visibility in both directions.
- Responsive suppliers are necessary to successful manufacturing because product life cycles are short and technological changes occur at a rapid pace. Shorter product cycles and shorter lead times mean that suppliers must be responsive to rapid changes in demand.
- Resilient and enduring relationships contribute to the efficiency of inbound materials management. This is often achieved by reducing the number of suppliers and coordinating supplier inventories with manufacturer inventory.

On-time, in-full, and error-free service is measured by comparing actual real-time quality and delivery from a supplier to a "perfect order." The perfect order is one that is delivered on-time and error-free 100% of the time.

The mathematical formula used to measure supplier performance is as follows:

A x B x C = Supplier Performance

- A: Represents the percentage of material orders with on-time delivery
- B: Represents the percentage of material or component orders meeting all manufacturer expectations
- C: Represents the percentage of material and component deliveries which are error-free

Consider a supplier that delivers its components to a manufacturer on time 85% of the time, in full 90% of the time, but delivers error-free orders only 60% of the time. Such a performance is likely to leave a company looking for another supplier(s).

Improvements in documentation and labeling would significantly improve overall performance, and can easily be achieved through better communications and technology.

AQL

AQL is the acronym for acceptable quality level. It refers to batches of products deemed acceptable for use in a manufacturing process. AQL is not the same as 100 percent inspection.

100 percent inspection is not practical for large batches of small parts. 100 percent inspection is costly and time consuming. It is suitable only for small volumes of expensive parts or components.

AQL inspection tests quality by examining small samples of large batch items. If a certain number of assembly bolts is taken from a sample lot and examined, and too large a percentage is found to be defective, the entire lot will be rejected.

On the other hand, if only an insignificant number of bolts from the control sample are examined and found to be defective, the entire batch will be rated as having an Acceptable Quality Level (AQL).

The chief weakness of the AQL method of inspection is that it does nothing to remedy the process variation of the defective parts.

- The AQL process only identifies the defects. If too many defective parts are discovered, the batch will be rejected and returned. This process is time consuming, expensive, and adds no value.

Another weakness of AQL inspection is that a company is paying for a certain (albeit small) number of defective parts, even for those batches which meet the standard.

A third weakness of the AQL inspection method is that, in accepting the quality level of a batch of parts, the defective small parts will be cycled to the assembly line, where each must be sorted out before they induce additional manufacturing problems. A company runs the risk of dissatisfied customers in the downstream segment of the supply chain.

Paperwork Reduction

Manufacturing activity will always generate paperwork, no matter how small the operation. However, even small organizations can be choked with unneeded and distracting documentation, much of it repetitive or overlapping. Reducing paperwork should be an ongoing effort in all organizations. Paperwork reduction contributes to morale as well as efficiency.

Paperwork reduction programs must be developed in concert with outside agencies and suppliers.

Orders from suppliers can be delivered in standardized containers to cut down on paper documentation. Consider the shape and size of an egg carton. One knows that a carton of a certain size contains a dozen of eggs. If you open the carton, it is immediately noticeable if one egg is missing. The shape and design of the container tells you this. This type of standardized containerization can be used to deliver a variety of parts or components.

Paperwork reduction programs must be developed in concert with outside agencies like suppliers. Manufacturers can work with vendors during the certification process to develop standardized containers that make it easier to gauge WIP and inventory.

- Standardized containers should be identical and contain a specified number of parts. They should be designed in such a way that items are visible. Egg carton and firearms cartridge packing are metaphors for larger standardized containers used for a variety of manufacturing purposes.
- Empty containers trigger replenishment. Exceeding a specified number of containers means an overstock of inventory.

When materials are too bulky or irregularly sized, it may be impossible to use standardized containers, so deliveries cannot always be standardized. It is best to minimize deliveries of these types of materials because they account for a large portion of inventory carry costs, usage of facility space, and handling costs.

Workpack Documentation

The amount of documentation that must accompany work flowing through an assembly or manufacturing process can vary according to the size of the company, the type of products it produces, and the complexity and number of steps in the manufacturing process.

- The degree to which outside suppliers or vendors are involved can add to or subtract from documentation requirements.
- In repetitive manufacturing where single, non-complex products are being manufactured in the same way, in the same amounts, and for the same purposes, the documentation requirements are lighter than in processes which are more specialized.
- Documentation requirements can be significantly more voluminous and detailed in a batch environment which manufactures products to different specifications with regard to the product itself, its packaging, and its level of demand.

Shop Packet

The amount of documentation enclosed in the shop packet depends on the complexity of the manufacturing process. Typical shop packet components may include:

- The manufacturing order: This details the product itself, the quantities and specifications to which it must be manufactured, and the destination of the part or product after manufacture.
- The picking list: This details the parts or components to be released from storage for the manufacturing to begin. It includes issue dates consistent with other scheduling.
- The bill of materials: This is included when the parts or components used are in excess of those coming from the parts store.
- Routing sheets: These are very detailed in many cases and, aside from showing progression from one work station to another, they provide additional instructions, set-up times, and run times.
- Manufacturing instructions: These may resemble routing sheets in some ways, but typically have specialized instructional guidance for complex assembly tasks. Manufacturing instructions may include drawings and a step-by-step graphic showing the way products are to be assembled.
- Tooling requisitions: These are most often issued by computer so as to eliminate errors that sometimes occur in manually-processed requisition issues.
- Move tickets: These are computerized documents that save manual entry (and time) on the shop floor.
- Labor tickets: These record the number of hours spent on the manufacturing order before the completed assembly is passed to a data capture operator.

Streamlining Documentation Requirements

Paperwork and product support documentation requirements serve a specific and useful purpose, but most often they do not add value to the finished product. Documentation is necessary, however, and decision about what types of paperwork must be maintained and which can be abandoned can be made by asking a few simple questions. Is the documentation necessary? Is the paperwork an unnecessary step?

Transaction costing analysis has shown that documentation overhead costs could be as high as 20% of total production costs. Among the potential remedies which can reduce paperwork are:

- Scheduling orders through vendors rather than through individual purchase orders can reduce paperwork.
- Having suppliers deliver straight to the work place will circumvent unnecessary steps in the receiving, inspection, and inventory storage areas.
- Kanban methods can reduce the amount of documentation required in the areas of work orders and scheduling.

Reducing Set-Up Times

Manufacturing analysts estimate that set-up time can be reduced by 30 to 50 percent by implementing universal practices like:

- Modifying and designing equipment to use standard and interchangeable parts and standardizing adjustment locations
- Ensuring that needed materials and tools are available before the setup begins
- Using videotaped sessions of set-up processes for training purposes
- Color coding standard connections like air, hydraulic, water, electrical, or other connections
- Directing tool and die designers to standard dies for quick-change operations
- For heavier or large dies or tools, setting feed table heights so that the tool(s) can be easily moved into the equipment slot
- Developing continuous and proper housekeeping habits to eliminate clutter and enhance organized and concerted manufacturing activity

A series of steps may be useful in evaluating the potential for setup time reduction in a manufacturing process.

- It must first be determined whether or not all steps in a manufacturing process add value. Steps which do not add value can be eliminated.
- Evaluating the potential for set-up time reduction can be accomplished by videotaping the process and studying the results.
- Improve the larger problems which cause larger delays first. Leave the fine-tuning and refinement for later revision.
- Prepare the work stations in advance of production activity. Check to see that all tools and standing inventory are in place. Check machinery for maintenance problems.
- Eliminate unnecessary material handling. Restrict the use of heavier equipment and use it to move heavier materials only.

Unnecessarily complex manufacturing processes result in longer set-up times. The simplification of a process isn't always easy to accomplish, but it can significantly reduce set-up times.

- Producing multiple varieties of the same product puts a strain on production changeovers, especially if the variations are of little consequence to the customer. For example, producing single, two-pack, four-pack, six-pack, and eight-packs of toothbrushes is costly if such variety is not needed. Two and six-pack production may satisfy the customer and reduce setup times.

- Excessive complexity in product variability sometimes has the effect of splintering the market without increasing overall market share. US automakers are increasingly following the Honda-Toyota model of producing different auto models on the same functional platform. This eliminates a great deal of setup, retooling, and changeover time.

SMED

The Japanese innovation of SMED (single minute exchange of die) is focused on reducing set-up times through analyzing the process and refitting the process with technology and better application of human resources.

- FMS, or flexible manufacturing systems, refer to the ability to quickly change the amount of produced items and the ability to produce variations of a specific product.
- SMED techniques are aimed at removing extraneous activities during set-ups by eliminating steps or combining activities to reduce the amount of time a machine must be stopped.
- SMED teams are convened to list all of the tools, supplies, equipment, and documentation that would be needed for a change-over and could be prepared in advance.
- SMED teams determine a priority list which sequences the activities that must be followed to achieve maximum efficiency.

Pipeline Time

Manufacturing lead time and pipeline management share the goals of lower costs, higher quality, and flexible manufacturing schedules, which allow facilities to respond rapidly to customer demand.

Pipeline management is a measurement of the amount of time a company's financial investment can be used to manufacture a product, deliver a product to customers, and receive a returned cash profit.

Pipeline time adds several additional metrics to lead time accounting:

- Inventory days of raw materials
- Number of days allotted to production
- Time occupied in transportation
- Time in order processing and replenishment
- Wasted time due to bottlenecks, deterioration, obsolescence, etc.

Manufacturing Schedule

The APICS definition of scheduling describes it as a way "to optimize the use of a resource to meet required production objectives at the lowest possible operating cost."

Schedulers would like to wave the magic wand and meet all scheduled dates and times, but real world scheduling does not work that way. Facility floor activities often compete and conflict with each other, delaying input and output. There are some general guidelines to follow in scheduling:

- The scheduling must be realistic and suitable to the type of work being performed.
- The scheduling system must be flexible enough to allow for correction of problems which develop.
- The scheduling must be purposeful. The purpose of scheduling is to meet objectives, not to keep machines and people busy in the hope of creating a "feel-good" environment.

- Schedules must be accurately communicated throughout the plant facility.
- Schedule reporting must provide useful and up-to-date information to overall management.

Cycle Time, Throughput, TOC

These terms are commonly used when analyzing manufacturing process flow with the objective of leaning the flow line.

- Cycle time is the length of time required to complete a process. It is a typical measurement used to assess flow line efficiency. Cycle times can be reduced by eliminating non-value adding steps and waste.
- Throughput is a figure representing the amount of manufacturing output of a process. It is measured based on a specific period of time: hours, days, weeks, etc.
- TOC is the abbreviation for Theory of Constraints. The theory maintains that performance improvement can only be accomplished by successfully addressing the part of the manufacturing process which causes the underperformance. Proponents of this view often argue that inventory buildup hides or disguises the root problems.

Throughput Efficiency

Throughput efficiency can be calculated by dividing the amount of Value Added Time by the End to End Pipeline Time and multiplying by 100 percent.

$$Throughput = Value\ Added\ Time \div End\ to\ End\ Pipeline\ Time \times 100\%$$

The elements in the supply chain which decrease throughput efficiency are:

- Excessive setup and changeover times as new product manufacturing begins or new versions of older products are manufactured.
- Bottlenecks in the flow of materials created by labor problems or by excessive inventory accumulation along segments of the supply chain.
- Poorly integrated order processing schedules.
- Poor communication and coordination along the pipeline as products move from end to end of the production sequence. This lack of visibility impairs the ability of operations management to take corrective action.

Floor Stock Reduction

Floor stock reduction is another way of increasing throughput and reducing overall cycle time.

- Economical use of floor space can be accomplished by using kanban systems and reducing order quantities. It may be desirable to set an upper limit on the amount of space that can be used and the amount of queued materials that can occupy it.
- Employing a use-one-order-one order process should be a goal of any floor stock reduction plan. Accomplishing this would reduce defects because problems with materials become more visible when bottlenecks are cleared from the production process.
- Research shows that floor stock reduction has a positive impact on flow line worker morale. This may account for increased throughput and cycle time reduction.

Decentralized Control

One of the chief goals of distribution planning is to use efficient administrative controls to achieve a high level of customer service within a cost ceiling.

Decentralized control of materials inventory distribution is one of two distinct and different policy measures to achieve this.

- The manager of a decentralized distribution chain operates independently. Such a manager is responsible for all the customers within the area or distribution network. The central distribution warehouse is run as if it is a separate business.
- Decentralized control assumes that stock is always available for replenishment. The manager employing this distribution method uses a stock replenishment plan based on time or stock level inventories. In other words, the manager sets reordering points according to weeks, months, or other time intervals, or by developing a system that will trigger reordering when a specific inventory count is reached.

CENTRALIZED CONTROL

Centralized control of inventory distribution is one of two distinct and different policy measures to achieve this.

- Centralized control of inventory distribution means that distribution is based on centralized demand forecasting. This means that the distribution planning manager distributes manufactured items to individual distribution centers based on the demand forecasts for each area.
- The central distribution planner coordinates distribution over the entire customer network and sends manufactured products to each distribution facility to meet projected demand.
- Centralized control of distribution makes use of time-based reorder points since demand forecasting is the basis of centralized material distribution planning.

Evaluating Performance and Providing Feedback

SPC

Statistical Process Control (SPC) is a term to describe the general methodology of using statistical methods and techniques to modify and control a production process, keeping the process and its output within predefined parameters through action based on statistical analysis, including distribution analysis, data pattern mining and tolerance reviews. One of the primary purposes of SPC is to reduce variation in the output and process, thus making the process more robust and resistant to variation of sub-processes due to mechanical wear, environmental conditions and myriad other real-world factors. SPC is invaluable from a quality inspection standpoint, because it is ultimately focused on quality control, which makes it simpler for inspectors to verify and investigate quality issues.

Implementing SPC requires the development of statistical charts, which are used to control the manufacturing process.

- A sampling is taken of all the specimens or items being produced.
- The samples are examined for defects and/or deviations from the required product specifications.
- The results of this testing are translated into range or percentage charts, or some other type of chart that lends itself to quick recognition of defect areas.
- As the defect areas are noted, identified, and isolated, the control specifications may be tightened. Adjustments to specifications are done to move towards producing a better quality product. Tolerances are typically shrunk until they are insignificant.

Causes of variation

In a statistical process control (SPC) environment, certain factors are taken into account during the analysis phase. These factors can be predicted based on the process and the nature of the system, such as mechanical wear, maintenance cycles, environmental changes and human error, and are known statistical factors. These factors are known as common causes of variation, because they and their general effects on a process can be predicted with a fair degree of accuracy, and are considered inside statistical control for this reason. Special causes of variation, on the other hand, are less subject to analytic inclusion because they are unusual or have effects beyond what statistical analysis can forecast. Special causes would include major accidents, natural disasters or rapid market shifts, and can at best be loosely approximated in SPC modeling, putting them outside of statistical control.

QFD

Quality function deployment (QFD) – a product design and development strategy focusing on identification and fulfillment of customer requirements through translating the voice of the customer (VOC) into technical terms and communicating those requirements to all staff with design input; QFD is closely associated with house of quality.

Standardization and simplification – a product design and development strategy used to design for manufacturability as well as eliminate time, process, and part waste in manufacturing through such practices as common routings, standardized production methods, consistent process cycle times (to avoid work in progress and queuing), minimization and commonality of parts used, factory synchronization, design and development based on existing components, reduction of complexity in operations, and more.

TQM

TQM stands for total quality management. An entire organization must be involved in the cross-functional team approach to quality management and continuous improvement of operations methodology. Consider the situation in which a single part breaks in an unusually high percentage of instances.

- Cost analysis employees must be brought into the process if a new part will be used to replace the old one.
- Marketing and sales personnel must communicate with customers to ensure that the substitution is acceptable.
- Quality control must determine whether the new part meets regulatory as well as quality standards.
- The engineering department must determine why the original part failed before designing the new part.
- Manufacturing personnel must be consulted to pinpoint any production problems which might follow the introduction of the new part.

Quality Specification Considerations

Global manufacturing has increased competition in supply chain networks around the world. It is more important than ever to deliver quality to the customer in the face of increased competition.

- Specifications and standards are increasingly important in setting the range of process variation.
- Process variations may be categorized as critical, major, or minor deviations from acceptable ranges.
- Quality specifications are becoming increasingly more demanding as orders for materials or components are sent to suppliers.
- Quality specifications can be specific to an industry, or they may be set by national or international standard setting agencies.

Better relationships between manufacturers and their suppliers have made it possible to implement higher specification quality standards before the materials or components are received at the manufacturing plant.

Quality Circle

A quality circle is a team of workers assembled for the purpose of maintaining quality improvement. A quality circle will meet often to propose solutions to common problems in the production process.

- The formation of quality circles is an organizational technique meant to promote employee involvement in high quality maintenance.
- Quality circles raise the level of quality awareness by applying peer group pressure on other workers. They also result in a higher skill level.
- Quality circles must be supported by top and middle level management.
- Quality circles must be voluntary. Effective quality improvement is more effective when workers make the choice themselves to participate in quality management groups.

Measuring Performance

An over reliance on financial measurements or those based strictly on cost analysis provides a restricted view of overall profitability. The best management approach is to combine financial and non-financial metrics.

Examples of financial performance measures:

- Short and long-term profits
- Total costs broken down into operating segments
- Dollar value of inventory
- Cost of storage inventory
- Overhead costs

Examples of non-financial performance measures:

- Size, location, and condition of physical inventory
- Customer service can be measured by order fill rate and response times
- Success or failure of product-mix decisions
- Evaluation of product steps to eliminate steps which add little or no value

Direct Labor Measurement

Traditional direct labor measurement was over concerned with efficiency and capacity utilization. The broader reach of modern direct labor measurement is directed toward meeting company objectives by applying the workforce to the performance plan. It is important to measure the direct labor costs noted below and integrate those with indirect labor cost savings:

- Number of alteration notices per product
- Number of units produced
- Number of receipts for stockroom transfers of materials and parts
- Number of direct labor hours used
- Total number of hours required for set-up
- Hours spent in quality inspection, in and out
- Facility hours of operation
- Number of customer complaints addressed

Less visible indirect costs that can be improved include poor communication, delayed or careless accounting practices, and customer service departments that do not recognize the Pareto Principle.

Quality Measurement

Four problems related to quality that must be constantly measured are:

- Inferior quality: Quality deficiency accounts for costly rejections and reordering of subassemblies, parts, or finished goods.
- Mistakes in documentation: Paperwork errors have a great impact on the assembly plant floor, as erroneous data may be promulgated throughout the communication system lines, causing problems far down the line from the location where the errors occurred.
- Machine downtime: Equipment failures are a problem that can defeat the purpose of extremely meticulous planning and scheduling.
- Factory yields: Production which is inconsistent with demand will cause inventory buildup or stockouts, both of which can hurt the "bottom line."

Production managers must work within the context of a continuous improvement philosophy. Quality measurement is a way of controlling problems. Successful quality measurement means continuously taking quality measurements of various parts of the production process.

- Machine downtime must be monitored. The purpose of measuring downtime is to isolate the causes which can be controlled so that they can be addressed separately from the elements which cannot.
- Customer order entry error information should be immediately passed on to the controlling personnel so that it can be reviewed and corrected before it hits the factory floor.

Defects of parts and components should be measured through constant sampling, with the information reflected back to suppliers. Communicating with a smaller number of suppliers is easier than communicating quality information to a large and disparate number of suppliers.

A lot of manufacturing suffers from a myopic, short-term view of production activity. Instead of working within the context of a continuous improvement philosophy, many managers are content to focus on short-term remedies for problems that repeatedly emerge.

Internal and External Customers

The term "customer" applies to the personnel within a manufacturing facility as much as it applies to the customers who order finished products. Both types of customers must be satisfied. Both must have materials and products delivered within expected lead times. Both expect high quality production and products.

- The internal customer is the next person or next work station on the flow line. That person or work station has an expectation of receiving a component, part, or partly-finished product that is high quality and has zero defects.
- An internal customer can also be another division or another assembly plant in the same company. That division expects products to be delivered on time and in the anticipated condition.
- The external customer is the one who returns financial profit to the producer upon receiving a high quality product within a specified timeframe.

Customer and Performance Metrics

Performance and customer satisfaction measurements are essential management tools in manufacturing. When establishing a set of performance or customer metrics, it is important to take a broad view, not a myopic one.

Customer metrics set parameters related to customer demand, needs, and satisfaction. Customer metrics can determine the effectiveness of delivery plans. Customer metrics are always based on the "perfect order," which is the delivery of the exact product, to the exact location, within specified time constraints, 100% of the time.

Performance metrics are focused on such elements as cycle-time reductions, set-up times, machine down times, operating times, inventory management, and a host of other tools.

Assignable Cause

Assignable cause is an attribute of quality control which stipulates that process variation is always present, occurs randomly, and has at least a small impact on every outcome of the process.

- Assignable cause may be traced with due diligence to any phase of a manufacturing system.
- Assignable cause is a quality control consideration wherein the source of process variation is isolated and identified.
- Assignable cause refers to a process which is unstable and will produce a process variation which exceeds tolerance thresholds.
- An example of the type of process variation for which managers must find an assignable cause would be a drilling machine with bearings worn enough to make the "bit" wobble slightly and drill holes larger than specifications intend as a result.

Common Cause

The key difference between common and assignable cause is that, while both can produce process variation, common cause variations will not significantly affect production outcomes.

- Common cause conditions of manufacture indicate that a process is stable and consistent enough to produce according to specifications. Batches and lot sizes of manufactured widgets will have process variation due to machine wear or perhaps environmental factors. However, the manufactured output will fall within established threshold tolerances, which allows for the delivery of quality products to the customer.
- Assignable cause refers to a process which is unstable and will produce a process variation which exceeds tolerance thresholds. Action must always be taken to identify and remedy the source of the faulty manufacture.

Normal Distribution

Statisticians use the terms normal distribution and bell curve to describe a condition of process variability which falls within an expected range. Simply put, this concept means that all products manufactured will have slight and tolerable differences in characteristics. Even more simply put, no product is manufactured to perfect form and condition. However, some will be closer to specifications than others. Normal distribution is a means of sampling a batch of manufactured products and using the data to produce a graph or chart. The result is a chart (bell curve) which has the approximate shape of a bell with smooth outlines. In other words, a bell curve is symmetrical.

When products are manufactured and the results are such that they do not fit into the bell curve pattern, they are considered irregular, unsuitable, and outside the established specifications.

Statistical Process Control is a way of examining the production process and comparing it against normal distribution curves (charts), otherwise known as bell curves.

Customer Complaints

Measurable elements in the interest of quality improvement of customer complaint strategies include:

- The number of complaints can be easily monitored and charted. The number of complaints must be broken down into relevant categories, such as delivery problems, quality problems, mistaken order entry problems, or other categories.
- Product quality and defect issues must be measured to determine whether the causes can be attributed to the material source or to manufacturing assembly problems.

- Customer complaint personnel should operate in full cognizance of the Pareto Principle, the concept that the smallest population of customers with complaints absorbs the largest amount of customer service resources. To improve the process, measurement can focus on the number of problems that can be quickly and efficiently resolved to the customer's satisfaction.

PRODUCT COST MEASUREMENT

The APICS definition of product cost is geared toward three general categories.

- Labor cost can be computed by the simple method of calculating the number of hours required to produce a product and multiplying it by the labor hour rate.
- Material costs are comprised of the purchase price of goods and components, but sometimes also include receiving and storing costs. If only the purchase price of materials is considered in calculating material costs, the data can be obtained from the purchasing arm of the company.
- Overhead costs can be determined using simple or complex methods. The simpler methods of accounting for overhead do not encompass many of the hidden costs of production and storage.

DIRECT COSTS AND INDIRECT COSTS

Cost accounting is an important measure of company profitability. Material, labor, and overhead costs make up total product cost, but it is often necessary to trace or break these costs down even further.

- Direct costs are costs that can be traced to a given cost object. These costs may be attached to a particular product, project, or department.
- Indirect costs are those which cannot be traced to a cost object in an economically feasible way. Indirect costs are often called overhead costs.
- A cost object is the term applied to any activity, component, part, or object for which separate cost data is compiled.
- A cost object is different than a cost driver. A cost driver is any factor or activity which, if changed, causes a change in the total cost of a related cost object.

OVERHEAD

There are many activities associated with manufacturing and other industries that do not have any direct relation to the product or service provided.

- An activity may be classified as overhead when an order for a product comes into the purchase order processing center.
- Activities associated with the receiving of materials in storage dock bays are classified as overhead.
- Materials and component inspection is an activity classified as overhead. This includes testing for quality.
- Documentation processing of accounts payable is an overhead expense.
- Production scheduling is an overhead expense not directly connected to the product.
- Facilities maintenance costs are an ongoing overhead expense.
- Customer complaint department costs are an overhead expense.

Cost Management

Cost management is used as a tool of operational control, but it has other functions as well.

- Cost management analysts have a primary objective, which is establishing the true costs of a product manufacture.
- Cost management is a significant part of both planning and control.
- Cost management must occasionally focus on and project expenditures for the irregular manufacture of "one-off" items.
- Cost management is typically the concern of accounting and auditing organizations, but it is also considered by managers when decisions are being made.
- Cost management makes comparisons of actual costs and anticipated costs.
- Cost management is often tasked to project changes in expenditure resulting from speculative changes in material, labor, and overhead.

Accounting systems break costs down into pre-set categories.

There are many different approaches to the problem of costing in product manufacture. Common cost accounting processes are:

- Process costing provides a common denominator for work produced by breaking production activity down to a common equivalent unit. It might be the choice for an activity which produces a commodity: mining, oil refining, or chemical plants.
- Product costing is a method aimed at tallying the costs of a product or product group. Product costing assigns the costs of material, labor, and overhead to specific products or groups.
- Job order costing takes the point of view that costs are associated with job activities as opposed to products.
- Standard costing is a traditional method, which uses pre-determined unit costs to control manufacturing activity levels.

Standard Costing Systems

Standard costing systems use predetermined units of manufacturing processing time to measure work progress.

- The time and cost differences between the standardized work processing units and the actual time and costs are maintained in a variance account.
- Material, labor, and overhead are set as target goals.
- While standardized costing has the advantage of stabilizing manufacturing management costs of material and labor, it has the disadvantage of being highly inaccurate when an attempt is made to use it to standardize overhead costs.
- Materials Requirements Planning systems employ a cost roll-up to determine material, labor, and overhead costs for accounting purposes.
- Standard costs are typically re-calculated on a quarterly basis to account for inflationary moves in commodity prices and fluctuating currency exchange rates.

The calculation of overhead costs is not as reliable as standardized labor and material costs when the standard cost accounting method is used in manufacturing. Overhead accounting variances are noted in the following areas:

- Variable Overhead Efficiency Variance refers to the difference between actual usage and the allowed usage of the cost drivers.
- Variable Overhead Spending Variance represents the calculated difference between the actual costs and the expected costs of variable overhead. The assignment costs attached to cost drivers like production hours or labor hours exceed expectations and cause unfavorable variances.
- Production Volume Variance is the difference between assigned fixed overhead and budgeted fixed overhead costs. An unfavorable variance is when output volumes are less than budgeted output volumes.
- Fixed Overhead Spending Variance is the difference between actual fixed overhead and budgeted fixed overhead.

The most common variances in standard costing methods occur as the results of wages, material, and time.

- Material variances occur because of defective products, which generate wasted materials. The material budget is exceeded if the production process produces so much waste that more material is needed than was apportioned to the work order.
- Rate of wage variance occurs when a manufacturer must pay more than the standard pay rate for certain tasks. In that case, actual costs will exceed planned costs.
- Time variances are most alarming when they are unfavorable. Getting a job done in less time than the standard time assigned to it is regarded as a positive variance. Exceeding the standardized time allotted to a task is a negative variance.

Product Costing Method

The product costing method of cost accounting is used to evaluate WIP and the cost of finishing goods.

- Product costing is a traditional way of looking at costs in terms of material, labor, and overhead.
- Product costing is comprised of indirect and direct costs.
- Direct costs are made up of elements like labor and materials.
- Indirect costs refer to costs accrued indirectly in producing the product. Energy costs to power machinery would be an example, as would the costs of maintaining it.
- While the cost categories of such things as labor costs and building maintenance costs are clear, there are many factors that impact accounting, and these valuations must be consistently maintained. The company must enforce a policy of cost attribution within those areas of manufacturing where there may be confusion.

Job Order Costing

Job order costing is an accounting system that assigns costs to specific tasks in the production process.

- Assignment of cost is based on the individual order received.
- Job order costing is independent of accounting period cut-off dates.

- Job order costing methods carry the costs along with the location of the product. Costs accrue to the job or batch order and are carried in that category until the finished product is placed in finished goods storage. At that point, costs are transferred (with the batch) from WIP to finished product inventory.
- End of month WIP is equal to the sum of costs attributable to each unfinished work order.
- Accounting personnel may use either standard cost measures or actual costs when using the job order costing method.
- Overhead, material, and labor are separately tabulated.

SCS

SCS is the acronym for Standard Cost Systems, and ABC refers to Activity Based Costing. While SCS needs updating, it is still commonly used in manufacturing activity planning. One of the best ways to use SCS is to combine it with ABC.

- ABC's primary use has been in manufacturing, though it can be used in other types of companies.
- ABC results in better product costing for companies that have a significant amount of indirect product cost. It is very useful as an aid to product pricing. The disadvantage of ABC is that it functions better as a cost accumulation measurement system, rather than as a cost control system.
- Most companies can benefit from some combination of ABC and SCS. One possibility is the use of ABC for indirect costs and the use of an updated SCS for direct costs. A blend of the two systems that combines the superior control features of SCS and the better overhead calculations of ABC is also an option.

INVENTORY COSTS

There are three basic types of inventory costs. Each type has a different impact on production and profit margins.

- Carrying costs: These costs are assumed by the corporation while a product waits in inventory for consumption. Carrying costs include: insurance, pilferage, spoilage or other deterioration, costs of obtaining capital, and storage and handling charges.
- Ordering and set-up costs: There may be a large number of hidden costs associated with processing an order for products. Accounting departments incur charges, and there are delivery charges for parts and components. Orders may also be subject to inspection costs. The process of setting up equipment to manufacture products also involves large costs during the initial phases.
- Stockouts and back-ordered costs: Shipping back-ordered items is associated with higher costs. The cost of stockouts is loss of market share. Another type of cost, known as "chasing costs," refers to the resources spent in locating products held in inventory.

INVENTORY CARRYING COSTS

Warehouse costs include labor, occupancy, and average inventory. However, there are also other costs that may be less obvious.

- Inventory costs include the cost of financing the capital needed to purchase and maintain materials in storage.
- Materials and components held in inventory require insurance against loss or theft.
- Spoilage and deterioration accounts for significant losses in some industries.

- New product development sometimes incurs losses when product life cycles are shortened by new technological developments. Obsolescence is an added risk in the current era of rapid technological change.
- The cost of building maintenance, equipment maintenance, and security for warehouse facilities adds to inventory carry costs.

Stockouts and Back Order Costs

Stockouts and back-orders pose a significant obstacle to lean manufacturing objectives as the system compensates for lost sales.

- Retail customers, suddenly aware of product shortages, may over-order for their own outlets in the hope of receiving enough product to meet demand. This type of activity can cause production bottlenecks when supply and demand again reach a state of equilibrium.
- Factories may ramp up production to meet the sudden surge in demand, only to find themselves in an oversupply situation when demand subsides.
- Back ordered products often require expedited delivery, which results in higher transportation costs.
- Backordered supply incurs additional transactional costs as the number of hours required for documentation and monitoring increases.
- Chasing costs accumulate as worker hours are dedicated to locating and expediting floor stock that can be used to backfill orders.

Continuous Review System

One cost-savings measure for cutting down on documentation and ordering costs associated with supply replenishment is called continuous review and replenishment.

Continuous review and replenishment policies are the opposite of periodic (timed) replenishment systems.

In the continuous review method, replenishment is accomplished by setting inventory trigger levels. The length of time between ordering may vary, as in the following example:

- Suppose that the inventory trigger level or baseline inventory is 10,000 units. The re-ordering trigger is set so that reordering from suppliers occurs when the number of units held in inventory drops below 5,000, regardless of the amount of calendar time that has passed.
- In the continuous review model, the amount ordered is always the same: 5,000 units. The baseline number of inventory units must be set so that it is sufficient to meet maximum production output demands.

Periodic Review System

A periodic method of inventory review is one in which the reordering cycle has a fixed time period, which triggers the re-order process.

- The time-based reordering triggers are set based upon specific intervals of time. The amount ordered during the interval of time may be variable or fixed.
- In special cases, and instances in which data can be rapidly communicated to suppliers, the amount ordered will be set at the amount that was consumed in manufacturing during a specified time period.

- Time-based reordering is desirable when the manufacturing facility must adhere to fixed or periodic ordering intervals that are required by the supplier.
- Time-based reordering is desirable when materials or components must be coordinated and distributed during the same time period, as in kitting.

Small order volumes with light demand cycles are more suitable to a time-based reordering system.

Inventory Accounting

Companies may do inventory on a continuous basis or periodically, according to the needs of the facility.

- APICS defines perpetual inventory accounting as an ongoing process that requires continuous data entry to update stocks. Some systems can automate this process, although there are usually considerable expenses involved. On the other hand, the manual entry and update of inventory stocks is time consuming.
- Periodic inventory accounting lends itself to use in small businesses. Stock is counted manually and replenishment orders are made when inventory stock reaches low levels. The disadvantage of this type of inventory accounting is that it can result in a highly irregular boom and bust cycle.
- Four-wall inventory accounting requires less storage, as raw materials and components move quickly to the locations where they are needed. Dedicated storage spaces aren't needed, and materials handling is minimal.

Cycle Inventory

Cycle inventory is the term applied to the average lot or batch size in a production process. It is the amount of inventory that must be held in stock to meet demand.

Cycle inventory is held to take advantage of economies of scale, either on the production side or on the purchasing side. On the purchasing side, the customer almost always takes advantage of larger batch sizes to gain cost advantages per unit.

Vendor Managed Inventory

The implementation of VMI, or Vendor Managed Inventory, methods can reduce in-bound lead times significantly. VMI requires the existence of a cooperative working relationship with suppliers.

- VMI shifts the responsibility for inventory management and supply replenishment to the supplier.
- A shift to VMI is accomplished through information sharing between the customer and the supplier. The customer may share an informational database of consumption rates and sales.
- The supplier is part of the replenishment system, and can access the data in real time rather than waiting for customer order documentation from the customer-manufacturer.
- VMI not only reduces documentation costs for the manufacturer, but also increases speed of delivery because it minimizes inventory bottlenecks. It does require suppliers who are certified for timely delivery of quality materials.

Minimizing Costs

Documentation and transactions do not add value to cars or television sets, nor to any other product. While transactions must be documented, it is important to reduce the amount of time and money spent to support operations which backlog systems without adding to profitability.

- Instead of taking individual purchase orders, it may be wiser to adopt a vendor scheduling system.
- Reducing the number of suppliers will reduce transactions and paperwork. It is easier to communicate with fewer suppliers, who can be instructed to deliver materials directly to the workplace.
- Kanban can replace scheduling and work orders on the assembly line.
- Integrating floor stock and back flushing techniques can reduce inventory accounting, order picking documents, and materials handling instructions.

Customer Service and Profitability Measurement

In order to be successful, companies must continuously review their metrics in two broad categories: customer service improvement and profitability improvement.

Improved customer service measurement includes categories of quality, delivery time, lead time reduction, and increased productivity. All of these single elements contribute to improved customer service, which is aimed at keeping and expanding market share.

Profitability measurement is aimed at a product's true value, a value obtained by evaluating all costs associated with the product's manufacture: utilities, clerical support, indirect labor costs, and others. By allocating costs related to specific products through ABC costing, business decisions can be made with regard to pricing. The least expensive product is not always the one that retains and builds market shares. Companies like Sony often price their products (LCD TVs) higher, but still have a dominant position in specific markets.

Delivery Performance Measurement

Delivery performance measurement is directed toward improving supplier relationships through better service. The criteria by which delivery performance is measured include:

- Responsiveness to customers should be an area of concern for the supplier. The supplier must evaluate its performance against known benchmarks and quality standards.
- Order entry processes work best when personnel who are knowledgeable and courteous when orders require clarification complete these processes.
- On-time delivery can be measured with a computation of SL or Service Level.
- Quantity control practices of the supplier can reduce work, time, and cost, and can improve lead times for manufacturers.
- Product condition should be of the quality anticipated when the order was made.
- Documentation must be accurate, but not redundant. It should be easy to locate the necessary information or special instructions accompanying materials delivered by suppliers.

OTIF

Some measurement of OTIF will serve as the basis for determining whether an external supplier can supply the flow lines of a manufacturer seeking a reliable supplier partnership.

OTIF means on-time and in-full. Delivery expectations have been met and the order has been filled within specified time constraints and according to the factory's specifications.

Another condition of certification added to the OTIF objective is error-free service. This means that the material or subassembly component labeling contains no address or content errors, packaging is intact and appropriate, and necessary shipping documents are provided.

Quality costs

Quality costs are those expenditures aimed at improving material quality and the manufacturing process. The statistics comparing US figures and those from Japan are striking. Clearly, companies can become increasingly competitive by focusing on quality cost reduction.

Quality costs can be classified as preventive costs, internal and external failure costs, and costs of inspection and appraisal.

Quality costs in Japan are in the statistical range of 5 to 10 percent. Quality costs are in the range of 15 to 30 percent in the US, where a great deal of money is spent on product failure related to warranty claims and litigation.

Clearly, the opportunity for better management and competitiveness is evident in these statistics. A first step toward better control of quality costs should be to prioritize the areas where quality cost reduction will provide the largest competitive dollar advantage.

Per-unit cost

One of the metrics that companies use to obtain a cost advantage in manufacturing markets is the per-unit cost.

- Per-unit costs are typically higher in the earlier stages of factory production, but decrease when the experience curve shows that the bugs have been worked out.
- The volume of product produced and the experience curve work together to produce a per-unit cost, the amount of money required to manufacture a single unit of a single product.
- Per-unit costs are the direct costs of production, although some accounting departments factor in overhead, insurance costs, and facilities costs into the computation.
- The cumulative volume of goods produced is related to the per-unit cost. A plastic mold that is used only 100 times to manufacture a plaster statue has a higher-per unit cost than a plastic mold that is used 1000 times before it is replaced.

CCC

The CCC, or cash conversion cycle, is the time it takes for a company to receive an order, manufacture it, deliver the product, and receive cash payment. A short cash conversion cycle indicates that there is efficient use of the plant, equipment, and inventory to meet customer demand.

- A short cash conversion cycle means leaner inventories, and ensures reliability on the supplier side. Excess inventory is costly. A steady and reliable flow of materials and components is required for competitive manufacturing.

CCC is a measure of how effectively a company's plant and equipment are utilized.

- A standard formula for computing CCC is:

$$CCC = DIO + DSO - DPO$$

where:

DIO – days inventory outstanding

DSO – days sales outstanding

DPO – days payable outstanding

Inventory Review Methods

Periodic inventory review means that a company reviews and replenishes its inventory according to a periodic and pre-determined schedule. Periodic review intervals may be daily, weekly, monthly, quarterly, or any other period of time which supports the manufacture. The advantages of periodic review are:

- Easier administration
- Orders arrive at convenient times where acceptance can be scheduled
- Fixed pickup or delivery times
- Ordering of multiple items can be grouped together

Continuous review of inventory also has its advantages. Continuous review of inventory is affected when a company sets minimum stock levels that must be met by its supplier. When the stock inventory dips below a certain number point, a replenishment order is triggered. The advantages of this method are:

- Less safety stock has to be maintained in inventory.
- Lot sizes are fixed and easier to handle since they are usually smaller.
-

LIFO and FIFO

One of the most important decisions business owners must make is how to measure their inventory.

- Inventory coming into a company has a fixed value, which is the value it had when it first arrived at the manufacturing plant. The manufacturing process adds value to the raw materials, and the product is then put into the finished goods inventory.
- LIFO stands for Last In – First Out. It is a method of inventory accounting which presumes that materials are used in the opposite order in which they are received. In other words, the material first-in is used last.
- FIFO stands for First In – First Out. It is a method of inventory accounting which presumes that materials are used in the order in which they are received. In other words, the materials first-in are used in the first manufacturing runs.

In the world of manufacturing, no matter what financial accounting method is used to value inventory, physical inventory often builds up so that several layers of inventory are held at the same time. Calculating the cost of that inventory would appear to be simply a matter of adding up the value of all the finished products held in inventory and then adding to it the value of all the materials in unfinished inventory. It is, however, far more complicated than that.

- Inventory accounting consists of tabulating beginning inventory at a chosen point, and also involves considering new materials, purchases and deliveries, finished goods inventory, the cost of goods sold, and the ending inventory.
- The implications of the chosen method of inventory accounting are of extreme importance. LIFO and FIFO produce temporary differences in accounting numbers.
- Methods of inventory accounting are often chosen on the basis of tax liability. However, LIFO and FIFO must conform. If a company uses LIFO for tax accounting, it must use LIFO for financial reporting as well.

Slack Time

The master planning schedule can provide reasonable estimates of the amount of time needed to complete various processes, but actual process times may vary. The difference between the process calendar time and the actual time needed to complete a manufacturing assembly is called slack time. Successful production scheduling means that each process must be completed by the start date, the time the next phase is set to begin.

- When a process is completed ahead of schedule, the time difference is called slack time. When a process is behind schedule, some managers refer to it as negative slack time.
- Slack time is useful in setting production priorities, and can be calculated by formulas such as the critical ratio formula.
- Total slack is the amount of delay that a process can tolerate without affecting the established completion date.
- Free slack is the amount of time a single part of the manufacturing process can be delayed without impacting the start of the subsequent work step.

Slack time computations are helpful in setting work priorities that allow jobs to flow without impedance from one work center to another. It is extremely important that each assembly step proceed at the scheduled time and that the timetable for the entire project is adhered to.

- The slack time rule directing the sequence of job tasks can be expressed mathematically by the formula:

  (days left x hours/day) - standard hours left = priority of task

- The task with the lowest remaining slack time gets the highest priority treatment at the work center.
- The queue ratio (also called "compression") is expressed in the mathematical formula:

$$Queue\ Ratio = \frac{Remaining\ Slack\ Time}{Remaining\ Planned\ Queue\ Time}$$

Work Centers

A gateway work center refers to the area where a manufacturing process first begins. It is the first stop in the routing sequence. Downstream work centers are the production steps which follow the initial assembly step. Within the operations management policy of setting priorities, there are two common methods of setting priorities.

Shortest processing time is a way of sequencing the production so as to dispatch or finish those jobs which take the least amount of time and effort first. Accomplishing the simpler assembly tasks early leaves a large block of time to address the longer and more complex tasks, during which obstacles are more likely to be encountered.

FIFO is the abbreviation for "first-in, first-out." Under this system, the first materials which arrive in inventory are used in assembly. They are moved out as quickly as they arrive to prevent bottlenecks. The term was originally applied only to inventory, but current uses of FIFO are combined with kanban to produce greater efficiencies.

Lot Splitting

Lot splitting is defined by APICS as the process of dividing of a lot into two or more sub-lots and processing them simultaneously as separate lots. The reasons for doing this would be to shrink lead times or to expedite a smaller production run for delivery to customers.

- A simple lot splitting activity is called operation splitting. This means that a lot is broken down into smaller batches that are processed on different machines and run at close to the same time. Practically speaking, one of the batches might require additional set-up changes or spend time waiting in queue pending equipment availability.
- Order splitting is a method of splitting the batch to meet a specific customer demand, usually a demand for delivery. Urgent delivery means that one of the sub-batches may be more expensive to process, but the customer has agreed to meet the additional costs.
- Both types of lot splitting are more expensive than large batch size/ high volume production, which makes use of economies of scale. Lot splitting requires additional set-up time.

Loading

- Forward loading is defined as the process of loading excess workloads to a forward scheduled period. Inevitably, the scheduled load of materials and products moving downstream toward completion will exceed available capacity. When the forward loading process detects overload, the excess work is shifted into a future time period sequence.
- Backward loading is a different way of treating overloads; it shifts the work to an earlier start date. It begins with selecting the order farthest into the future. Work is then moved backwards to an earlier fixed start date.
- Infinite capacity loading is defined by APICS as a calculation of required capacity which does not take into account the ceiling capacity of work centers involved in the manufacture. Most MRP systems are based on this principle since it provides data which can be used to redirect and reschedule work overloads.

UPL

The concept behind Uniform Plant Load is represented by the maxim "If a company sells daily, it must build daily."

- Each model sold is assembled on a daily basis in relatively small quantities.
- Uniform Plant Load is the rate of production which can be sustained by a synchronous measurement of all component and assembly processes.
- UPL means that the only manufacturing completed is directly tied to orders received.

- UPL means that manufacturing of different components or products is done by breaking the day down into single-day quantities. Instead of devoting 10 days of the month to Product A and 20 days of the month to Product B, both product runs occur on the same day in a proportionate amount (2/3 of the day for Product B; 1/3 for Product A).

Within the process of UPL, production rates are not tied to machine rates or production capacity. The rate of production (drumbeat) is instead tied to demand pull.

- Instead of a make-to-stock environment, UPL is a make-to-order environment. UPL represents the demand per day divided by the hours available for production.
- UPL is equal to the cycle time required to match demand.
- UPL reduces indirect labor costs (management of excess inventory).
- UPL relies on cross-training and labor shifting so that workers will not be laid off, a common result of the valleys and peak periods that occurred in older-style manufacturing facilities.
- Proper application of UPL techniques will result in synchronized production volumes from work center to work center.

Task Times

Variability in task times has a great impact on the type of assembly line which may be effectively employed in manufacturing. In the real world, task time is never absolute. There are several different ways of viewing the problem of task times, however.

- Deterministic task times are a method of standardizing tasks and the times required to complete them. While the time to complete the actual task may vary from its calculated standard time, the deterministic method works when time differences are small and the task is simple and usually occurs without unpredictable delay.
- Stochastic task times are considered when there is a variety of worker response and individual skills are involved. These are often used in complex manufacturing processes in which there is significant variability in task completion.
- Dynamic task times are used when learning curves become a factor or there are large and progressive improvements in technology.

Deterministic task times are a method of standardizing the times required to complete tasks. While the time to complete the actual task may vary from its calculated standard time, the deterministic method works when time differences are small and the task is simple and usually occurs without unpredictable delay.

- Set the standard time for a single task by using observational data.
- Determine the production goals set for the day.
- Calculate the number of man hours needed by multiplying the time it takes to complete a single item by the number of items that must be produced per day.
- Divide the total number of man hours required by the number of man hours available.
- Once these simple computations are in place, the work can be apportioned on the balanced assembly line.

GANTT CHARTS

A man named Henry Gantt developed the specialized chart, which is a useful tool in scheduling.

- A Gantt chart is a horizontal bar chart which shows a time scale on the horizontal axis. The time scale may be in hours, days, weeks, months, etc.
- The vertical axis represents segmented blocks of time devoted to various assembly tasks. Vertical segments are numbered in terms of task sequence.
- Blocks of time occupied by various times are shaded or blocked out. The result is an easily understandable and visibly clear graph of activity.

The greatest advantage of the Gantt chart is its ability to display at a glance the status of each work task. Gantt charts can be readily constructed using common spreadsheet software like Excel and others. They can easily be sent via email using the popular and common ASCII text format.

COST CENTER AND COST DRIVER

The terms are popularly used in relation to Activity Based Costing, or ABC.

Cost centers are branches of a company which add to costs and expenditures, but do not directly add to profitability. Advertising and marketing departments are an example of cost centers. Research and development is expensive, but does not immediately add to profitability. Customer service is another example of a cost center.

A cost driver is any activity that results in a cost being incurred. The concept is useful in identifying the activities which cause indirect costs, which are costs that are incurred, but do not directly add to product value. A cost driver for maintaining safety on the work floor might be the number of dangerous machines or areas where forklifts operate.

The traditional view of cost driving held that production output requirements were the significant cost drivers. A change in business structures and increased technology added new dimensions to the manufacturing process. Activity based costing, or ABC, is a method of identifying cost drivers of specific activities.

Some examples of indirect costs and their drivers are:

- Maintenance costs are indirect costs. The driver of these activity based indirect costs may be the number of machines or the number of hours they are producing waste, for example.
- Raw material costs are direct costs. Handling and moving raw materials from storage inventory to the work cell is an associated indirect cost.
- The volume of orders received is another indirect cost driver of raw materials purchasing.
- Another ABC category may be inspecting incoming raw materials. The cost driver for this activity may the company's policy dictating the number of inspections.

FIXED AND VARIABLE COST

Total costs are made up of two components: fixed and variable costs.

- Fixed costs are those costs which do not vary with the volume level of activity. A warehouse's rent and utility costs will remain the same, whether the warehouse is full or half full. Material handling costs may vary according to the amount of volume moved, but that is a variable cost.

- Variable costs change in relation to the level of activity. Variable costs are those that are affected by such elements as production volumes or sales demand. A firm that manufactures jewelry must purchase commodities like gold, silver, or jewels at variable prices.

Control Charts

A control chart is a graph of sample data taken from manufacturing output. It is used to determine when the process variation is sufficient to fall into the area of assignable cause, or special cause, as some people call it.

- Control charts have an Upper Control Limit and a Lower Control Limit.
- The Upper Control Limit is the calculated limit above the mean line. It should be placed 3 standard deviations above the mean.
- The Lower Control Limit is the calculated limit below the mean line. It should be placed 3 standard deviations below the mean.

The control chart is not to be used as a tool for controlling common cause variations, as this will waste time, and could exacerbate insignificant problems.

Control charts are used to monitor manufacturing quality. Control charts may measure a single quality (univariate) characteristic, or they may measure a characteristic having more than one quality (multivariate). If a single quality characteristic has been measured or computed from a sample, the control chart shows the value of the quality characteristic versus the sample number. The chart contains a center line that represents the mean value for the process being examined. Two other horizontal lines are drawn. The top line is called the upper control limit (UCL) and the lower line represents the lower control limit (LCL). These control limits are chosen so that almost all of the data points will fall within these limits.

Risk Analysis Scoring System

FMEA risk analysis scoring systems are devised to assign numerical values to the probability of failure in various phases of the manufacturing process.

The severity of failure is the most important concern.

Severity of failure may be evaluated by assigning numerical values to a range of possible effects. For example:

- Use the number one (1) for a process failure event which will have no impact on the process or service.
- Use the number two (2) for a failure event which may cause a temporary bottleneck in production or service.
- Use the number three (3) for a failure event which will have a major impact on production, and will likely affect profitability.
- Use the number four (4) for an event which will not only affect profitability, but will also halt the business for an extended period of time.

By assigning numerical values to failure events, production processes may be separated out for re-engineering or re-design.

SPC

The use of statistics to manage a process in manufacturing is called Statistical Process Control. Frequent, random samples of industrial output are taken and then tested against a normal distribution curve to determine the level of process variance.

- SPC can benefit process manufacturing because it looks at quality at the source.
- SPC provides objective rather than subjective data to support the decision-making process.
- SPC abets DRIFT manufacturing (Do It Right the First Time) by providing the tools to correct production process problems before they reach the customer.
- SPC reduces process variation and ensures that products are manufactured to meet high quality standards.
- SPC results in a sense of worker pride, job satisfaction, and accomplishment.

TAKT TIME

Takt Time is another concept derived from Japanese manufacturing. Takt Time is a measurement of the ratio between the desired rate of production and customer demand.

- Demand is variable, but modern forecasting methods have made it more predictable. A common demand measurement in the auto industry is the number of days an auto remains in inventory at the dealership before being sold.
- Toyota reviews Takt Time each month for products it manufactures, and adjustments of production are made even more frequently.
- To calculate a desired rate of production, demand must be divided by available time for manufacture. For a factory that operates 40 hours per week:
- Takt Time = Demand / 40 hours = X units per hour
- Supposing that demand is 100 units (cars?) in forty hours:
- 100 cars/40 hours = 2.5 cars per hour
- 2.5 cars per hour is the desired production rate or Takt Time.

In order to calculate the number of workstations required to meet Takt Time requirements, we take the sum of the cycle times of each step and divide that by the Takt time. A formula for that calculation would look like this:

$$\mathrm{W_{Min}} = \frac{\sum_{i=1}^{I} T_i}{\text{Takt time}}$$

It is sometimes necessary to calculate the amount of idle time absorbed into a process. To account for these times, there is a formula for calculating idle time:

$$W_{Actual} \times CT - \sum_{i=1}^{I} T_i$$

Takt Times cannot be improved. The only way of approaching Takt time efficiency is to reduce cycle times and eliminate wasteful and non-value adding steps. Setup time reductions would also help, as would better managed constraints.

CPIM Practice Test

Want to take this practice test in an online interactive format?
Check out the online resources page, which includes interactive practice questions and much more: **mometrix.com/resources719/cpimeco**

1. The most accurate statement regarding per unit costs of a manufactured item is that

a. The per unit cost increases in the later stages of a manufacture because of fatigue, inventory buildup, and bottlenecking
b. The per unit cost is reduced when smaller volumes are manufactured
c. The per unit cost never includes overhead costs
d. The per unit cost is typically higher in the earlier stages of factory production

2. The three basic types of inventory cost are:

a. Cost of financing, cost of materials, cost of management and labor
b. Carrying costs, order and setup costs, stockouts, and backorder costs
c. Chasing costs, setup costs, and finished product storage
d. Maintenance costs, moving equipment costs, and warehousing costs

3. The four primary activities of operations management planning are:

a. RCCP, MRP, MPS, and distribution planning
b. Inventory, operations, financial, and information management
c. Process costing, product costing, standard costing, and job order costing
d. Job shop environment planning, batch planning, flow line planning, and continuous manufacturing planning

4. The three primary levels of management in manufacturing planning and control (MPC) are

a. Lead times, capacity requirements, and capacity testing
b. Procurement, kanban, and production management
c. Top management planning, operations management planning, and operations management execution
d. RCCP, MRP, and MPS

5. The phase of MPC that includes sales, operations, and resource requirements planning is:

a. Operations management execution
b. Operations management planning
c. Top management planning
d. All of the above

6. Among the four statements below, the incorrect or FALSE statement is:

a. Capacity testing is done during OMP, or operations management planning
b. OMP includes scheduling and material requirements planning
c. Kanban streamlining is done during the top management planning phase of MPC
d. Time frames for production are set during the top management planning phase of MPC

7. In the beginning stages of planning, sales and operations are linked because:

a. The rate of production is set in accordance with projected sales
b. Senior management must determine products and product families far into the future and set production schedules that maximize production capacity
c. The production plan must identify product volumes at specific time periods to account for seasonal or other periodic fluctuations of sales
d. Of all of the above

8. How does RRP enhance and balance manufacturing operations?

a. RRP ensures more efficient material distribution through the employment of kanban techniques
b. RRP balances material needs to productive capacity and tests operational planning and performance
c. RRP allows for better senior management planning of sales and operations.
d. RRP disperses manufacturing data throughout all work centers involved in a manufacturing process

9. The timeline for manufacturing and sales is sometimes called the "planning cycle." During each planning cycle, managers of both sales and operations meet to discuss:

a. Inventory levels, seasonal demand fluctuations, monthly and quarterly production scheduling
b. Inventory handling, storage, shipping costs, and spoilage
c. The costs of maintaining inventory, manufacturing costs, and overhead
d. All of the above

10. APICS defines the master production schedule (MPS) as a set of figures and projections used as the basis for materials requirements planning. The MPS differs from forecasting in that:

a. It depends heavily on demand forecast figures, availability of material, and management policies
b. It puts greater emphasis on forecasts of both trend variation and seasonality than on specifics
c. The master production schedule is specific with respect to the configuration of product groups to be manufactured, the quantities to be manufactured, and the target dates for beginning and completion
d. All of the above

11. Kanban is an inexpensive method of manually balancing inventory supply and preventing work center bottlenecking. One very simple method is called the kanban square. The best description of a kanban square is:

a. A square card that, depending on color, signals replenishment must be done
b. A painted square on the factory floor that, when empty of supply, signals replenishment must occur
c. A completed batch of finished product placed in the square area allotted to finished inventory
d. A colored box that, when empty, signals demand for more upstream supply

12. Of three different production process configurations, the one that moves unfinished products to different work centers on the basis of work function is:

a. Fixed site production
b. Job shop
c. Flow shop production
d. Batch production

13. How does RRP work to reduce inventory and control production?

a. Senior management uses RRP to fit manpower to workloads, to develop schedules for materials routing and production, and to fine-tune lead times.
b. Senior management uses RRP to develop a generalized plan for materials routing and production and for refining lead times.
c. Senior management uses RRP to develop accurate demand forecast data.
d. Senior management uses RRP to balance actual demand with projected sales.

14. Make-to-stock, assemble-to-order, and make-to-order are parts of a manufacturing company's:

a. Sales strategy
b. Scheduling strategy
c. Positioning strategy
d. Production strategy

15. Low-volume manufacturing of custom-built products would likely occur in:

a. Flow shops
b. Continuous flow shops
c. Project manufacturing shops
d. Job shops

16. When the MRP logic system indicates additional personnel must be added to equipment capacity, operations managers choose to ask employees to work overtime.

a. The use of overtime hours is an inexpensive way to increase personnel capacity
b. The use of overtime hours can overcome equipment capacity limitations
c. Overtime work adds capacity but may be outside the limits of costs set for manufacture
d. The use of overtime hours is always preferable to other methods such as subcontracting

17. When capacity needs improvement to meet demand, viable options to the use of overtime hours include all of the following EXCEPT:

a. Alternative routing
b. Worker training
c. Subcontracting
d. New hiring

18. The statement that best defines alternative routing is:

a. A method of transferring backlogged work to different assembly paths on the shop floor
b. A method of transporting replenishment materials by alternative roads under certain emergency conditions
c. A computerized method of controlling the movement of product data that feeds directly into inventory accounting
d. Routing unfinished product through a subcontractor assembly point

19. Which of the following is NOT a component of production activity control?

a. Subcontracting
b. Work loading
c. Production metrics
d. Work scheduling

20. The addition of personnel to add capacity to work centers may encounter obstacles such as:

a. Union rules and restrictions
b. Budget limitations
c. Equipment shortages
d. All of the above

21. The importance of the daily dispatch list in execution of manufacturing operations is that:

a. The daily dispatch list transmits production information from the production supervisors to the shop floor supervisors
b. The daily dispatch list is essentially a price list of items at specific phases in the assembly process
c. The dispatch list sets stop and start dates and times for specific operational phases of items in the process of manufacture
d. All of the above

22. The characteristics of lot-based procurement are:

a. Ongoing commitment to the supplier for materials or component lots
b. Continuity of materials and/or component supply costs during the contract period
c. No ongoing commitment to the supplier after the purchase order contract is completed and the materials are delivered to specifications
d. Suppliers are responsible for the continuous flow of materials/components needed for manufacture

23. For continuous flow manufacturing entities needing standard raw materials or components to support production, the procurement choice is most likely to be:

a. Lot-based procurement
b. Procurement supply scheduling
c. The procurement release system
d. Flow shop procurement

24. A type of procurement that allows for both long-term and short-term supply flexibility is called:

a. Lot-based procurement
b. Procurement release system
c. Procurement supply scheduling
d. Flexible release scheduling

25. A load profile report calculates the utilization and efficiency of machines:

a. As if each machine center were a single machine
b. On an individual machine basis
c. With a large unit inventory as the standard
d. In fairly subjective terms

26. Manufacturers and suppliers may sometimes coordinate their efforts in relationships characterized as:

a. Product positioning strategies, joint capacity management, input/output control partnerships
b. Central supply planning, central distribution planning, operational partnering
c. Production planning, shipping cooperatives, capacity alliances
d. Strategic alliances, technical-commercial partnering, operational partnering

27. The difference between factory repair operations and remanufacturing operations is:

a. In remanufacturing, only worn or broken parts are replaced
b. In factory repair operations, it is easy to predict the need for raw materials or component parts
c. In remanufacturing, nearly all parts are restored to original "like-new" condition
d. In factory repair operations, products are generally returned with longer, extended warranties

28. Manufacturing design planning activity begins with a clear statement of objectives based on

a. Volume-variety characteristics and process type
b. Proximity of the manufacturing location to consumer market
c. Work cell layout and process charts
d. Competing market interests and cost of manufacturing

29. Of the four chief tasks in designing a cell layout for plant configuration, the component that determines equipment selection, setup and assembly time projections, and labor utilization is called:

a. Infrastructure design
b. Product selection
c. Process engineering
d. Work cell layout (SPU)

30. Color coding standard connections like air, hydraulic, water, electrical, or other connections used in the assembly process are an effective way of:

a. Decreasing setup times
b. Training workers in the use of equipment
c. Improving infrastructure design
d. Assisting operations supervisors in managing workers

31. Arrange the four categories of facility layout in ascending order beginning with the most expensive and ending with the least expensive.

a. Project layout approach, cell layout, product layout, process layout
b. Project layout approach, process layout, cell layout, product layout
c. Process layout, project layout approach, cell layout, product layout
d. Project layout approach, process layout, product layout, cell layout

32. The ideal outcome of synchronous manufacturing would be

a. A balanced assembly process in which all machinery and equipment is in operation according to scheduled run times
b. An assembly process in which all workers are performing the same task at the same time
c. An assembly process producing two or more products that are finished within synchronized lead times
d. A balanced assembly process where input of raw materials and components is equal to output of finished product

33. Put the following elements into sequential order: detailed scheduling at the CRP level or PAC level; master scheduling daily or weekly; MRP low level manufacturing schedules; production plan from operations and sales; order scheduling by materials requirements planners.

a. Detailed scheduling at the CRP level or PAC level; master scheduling; MRP low level manufacturing schedules; production plan from operations and sales; order scheduling by materials requirements planners
b. Order scheduling by materials requirements planners; detailed scheduling at the CRP level or PAC level; master scheduling; MRP low level manufacturing schedules; production plan from operations and sales
c. Master scheduling;detailed scheduling at the CRP level or PAC level; MRP low level manufacturing schedules; production plan from operations and sales; order scheduling by materials requirements planners
d. Sales and operations production plan; master schedule daily or weekly; lower level manufacturing planning by MRP; MRP order scheduling; detailed scheduling at PAC or CRP level

34. The statement that best explains the manner in which backflushing contributes to the desired balance of input and output in the greater efficiency and lesser waste of synchronous manufacturing is:

a. Backflushing refers to the process of moving defective products backward through assembly to correct and repair blemishes
b. Backflushing is a postproduction activity that draws supply from the BOM rather than from preproduction inventory storage
c. Backflushing is a way of optimizing system resources through backward scheduling
d. All of the above

35. Flow control scheduling would be best used in manufacturing ________.

a. That has all manufacturing machines grouped in work centers
b. In which smaller volumes of customized work take a variable path through different work centers
c. That produces large, complex, and multifaceted products like planes and ships
d. In which large volumes of materials flow in a set path toward completion

36. The forward loading method of dealing with excess workloads involves:

a. Shifting work to an earlier start date
b. Loading excess workloads to a forward scheduled period
c. Beginning with the work order farthest into the future
d. Staying within the ceiling capacities of all work centers

37. The backward loading method of dealing with overload is to:

a. Shift the work to a later, forward-scheduled date and time
b. Shift the work to an earlier scheduled start date
c. Move all the start times for all production schedules backward
d. Move all production start times forward

38. In forward scheduling with finite loading _______________.

a. The start date is flexible but the end date is fixed
b. Both the start and end dates are flexible
c. The end date is flexible, determined by the time it takes to manufacture the required quantity using available capacity
d. Work is loaded without regard for finite capacity

39. In backward scheduling with finite loading, _______________.

a. Both the start date and the end date are fixed
b. Both the start and end dates are flexible
c. Work is loaded without regard for finite capacity
d. The end date is fixed, and determines the schedule for backward loading

40. Of the statements below, the best description of process-oriented finite loading is:

a. Process-oriented finite loading makes efficiency gains from minimizing delays at individual work centers
b. Process-oriented finite loading seeks production efficiency gains by maximizing capacity utililization
c. Process-oriented finite loading seeks to improve production efficiency by planning around the constraints of bottlenecked work centers
d. All of the above

41. Which of the following statements is FALSE regarding the factory configuation termed the U-shaped flow line?

a. The U-shaped flow line facilitates communication and visibility among workers
b. The U-shaped flow line allows for each worker-machine unit to perform different manufacturing tasks
c. U-shaped work cells can easily be configured to produce different products with the same family group
d. The U-shaped work cell saves floor space and shortens material movement distances within the cell

42. The QRM style of flow line manufacturing relies on _______________ as the basis for designing the individual phases of work within each cell.

a. Visibility and communications
b. Variable demand and finite loading
c. Level scheduling and takt time
d. Input and output volume

43. Takt time can be defined as:

a. A calculation of the setup time plus production time per unit of product
b. Acalculation of the minimum production time per unit allowed to produce a product
c. A calculation of the maximum production time per unit allowed to produce a product
d. A combined calculation of inventory handling, setup time, and production time per unit of product

44. A key difference between QRM and JIT is that:

a. Unlike JIT, QRM flow lines may be nonlinear
b. Unlike JIT, QRM flow lines are linear in configuration
c. JIT relies more heavily on flexibility, whereas QRM relies more heavily on takt time and level scheduling
d. QRM relies more heavily on kanban than JIT does

45. To make efficiency gains, quick response manufacturing (QRM) puts the emphasis on:

a. Inventory reduction
b. Kanban techniques
c. Lead time reduction
d. On-time delivery

46. The type of manufacturing customer best served by QRM is:

a. The customer who requires baseline products that do not have significant product variation
b. The customer needs custom-engineered items designed with a wide variety of product options
c. The customer who needs consumer products that require continuous replenishment and have a stable demand
d. Customers who retail identical consumer items on a large scale and volume

47. Paired-cell Overlapping Loops of Cards with Authorization (or POLCA) is:

a. A material control method
b. An inventory reduction method
c. A takt time reduction technique
d. A pull system

48. A modern manufacturing cell configuration can be described as having a "horizontal" structure because:

a. The labor unit of a modern cell configuration is cross-trained and highly skilled
b. There is no operational management hierarchy because skilled workers have control and ownership of the work
c. Machines and equipment within a cell are of different types
d. Of all of the above

49. Provide the mathematical formula for the cash conversion cycle (CCC) where DIO means days of inventory outstanding; DSO means days of sales outstanding; and DPO means days payable outstanding.

a. A standard formula for computing CCC is CCC = DSO + DIO – DPO
b. A standard formula for computing CCC is CCC = DSO – DPO + DIO
c. A standard formula for computing CCC is: CCC = DIO + DSO +DPO
d. A standard formula for computing CCC is CCC = DSO – DIO + DPO

Answer Key and Explanations

1. D: The correct answer is "d." Per unit costs are typically higher in the earlier stages of factory production, but decrease when the experience curve causes an increase in manufacturing efficiency. The volume of product produced and the experience curve work together to produce a lower per unit cost, the amount of money required to manufacture a single unit of a single product. Per unit costs are most often the direct costs of production, but some accounting departments factor in overhead, insurance costs, and facilities costs into the computation.

2. B: Choice "b" is correct. There are three basic types of inventory costs. Each type has a different impact on production and profit margins. Carrying costs are assumed by the corporation while a product waits in inventory for consumption. Carrying costs include insurance, pilferage, spoilage or other deterioration, costs of obtaining capital, and storage and handling charges. Ordering and setup costs entail costs accrued in setting up equipment to manufacture products. Stockouts and backordered costs are costs associated with insufficient supply of finished products.

3. A: The correct answer is "a." Operations management planning consists of rough-cut capacity planning. RCCP establishes maximum production capacity and maximum material and labor capacity. Materials requirements planning sets the stage for the production schedule. Master production scheduling sets the parameters for manufacturing the product, from raw material to finished product. Distribution planning is vital to operations management planning, and ensures that materials will be available to meet production schedules.

4. C: Answer "c" is correct. Manufacturing planning and control (MPC. occurs at three distinct levels or phases. Top management planning includes sales and operations planning, and resource requirements planning. During this process or phase, top managers set volume requirements by product groups and establish time frames for production. Operations management planning includes scheduling and material requirements planning, and also sets the parameters for capacity requirements. Capacity testing is done during this phase. Operations management execution refers to the control phase of MPC, during which plans are executed.

5. C: The correct answer is "c." Top management planning includes both sales planning, operations planning, and resource requirements planning. During this process or phase, top managers set volume requirements by product groups and establish time frames for production. During the top management planning stage, the task is to create an overall blueprint for the manufacturing operation. Long-range financial and marketing concerns are addressed and an aggregate of supply channels are selected to enable the corporation to reach profit goals.

6. C: The correct answer, that is, the FALSE statement is shown in "c." Kanban refers to a method of streamlining factory assembly developed initially by the Japanese. Operations management execution refers to the control phase of MPC, during which plans are executed. Aside from kanban, other components of control are procurement, and actual assembly line or work center production. The procurement component involves negotiating the supply, transportation, handling, and storage of materials or parts needed for manufacture.

7. D: Answer "d" applies to early planning by senior management. One of the early planning tasks that must be addressed by the senior management team is a coordinated plan for sales and operations. Senior management must define the products and family groups to be sold and they must plan far into the future when material resources may fluctuate and meeting production schedules and sales targets become more difficult. Senior management must consider economies of scale as productive capacity comes close to its top levels. After coordinating sales and operations, the senior top management team must develop and distribute separate sales and production plans.

8. B: Choice "b" is the best answer, even though there are elements of truth in the other answer choices. RRP, or resource requirement planning, is a way of matching resources to production capabilities with a view toward greater efficiency of utilization. RRP can analyze and anticipate long-term material needs and requirements, balancing materials and capacity in a way that prevents shortages or bottlenecks in manufacturing. It also serves as a testing mechanism that validates the metrics of operational planning and performance. RRP relies heavily on computerization for the the transmission of data through the manufacturing environment.

9. A: The correct answer is "a." Sales and operations segments meet regularly to identify the needs of the organization and changing circumstances pertaining to the planning cycle. Among the issues that are addressed and discussed at regular planning meetings are inventory levels, seasonal changes in production and sales, discrepancies between forecasts and actual sales, product grouping and differentiation, and monthly/quarterly production scheduling. All of these elements fall within the reach of the "planning cycle" and can be adjusted to more accurately align production targets with product demand.

10. C: The correct answer is shown in option "c." Choices "a" and "b" represent coordinated areas that are common to forecast and specific data. The MPS is a specific set of figures and data that serve as a basis for MRP. Unlike forecast data, the master production schedule is specific with respect to the configuration of product groups to be manufactured, the quantities to be manufactured, and the target dates for beginning and completion. Standing inventory and "pipeline" inventory are also considered. Less predictable are forecast areas like availability of material and management policies.

11. B: Answer "b" is correct. Kanban is a concept used in the early days of Japanese auto manufacturing to signal increased demand to upstream suppliers. It is an inexpensive method of controlling excessive and costly inventories from bottlenecking work centers. The kanban square is simply a rectangle painted on the factory floor. Material needed for a manufacturing process is placed in the square for use in the work center. When the square is empty, the empty kanban square is the signal for replenishment of the part or component.

12. B: The question pertains to factory configuration so answer "b" is correct. Job shops are organized on the basis of work center function and move to different work centers for additional processing and finishing. Fixed site production is generally used to giant projects where supplies are delivered to the same place. Ship or airplane buildings are examples of fixed site production. Flow shop production is a type that has products moving along the same sequence of steps—rather like the traditional assembly line. Batch production is strictly an activity of manufacturing and not a mode of manufacture.

13. A: The best answer is "a." It is important to recognize that RRP is a combined strategy that employs a variety of computerized planning components and tools. RRP is both an inventory reduction plan and a production control plan that matches manpower to workload at specific points in the manufacturing process, establishes reliable lead times, and reworks production schedules to fit materials availability. In its final steps, RRP executes, monitors, and applies metrics to the production plan.

14. C: The correct answer is "c." The categories in question are the components of a manufacturing positioning category. Product manufacturing businesses classify their activities into two broad categories: positioning strategy and production process strategy. Both classifications are influenced by the product volumes intended for manufacture. For example, make-to-stock, a positioning strategy, is the best chioice for manufacturing of high volumes of consumer items with identical characteristics and specifications. Such items would likely be manufactured in a flow shop—a process category.

15. D: The correct answer is "d." Product manufacturing of lower volume that involves a higher degree of customization occurs in job shops or batch flow shops. This type of manufacturing provides the flexibility needed for customization. Higher volume manufacturing with a standard design is usually made in flow shops and made-to-stock. There is less flexibility in this type of manufacturing. Project manufacturing refers to the extreme opposite of high volume manufacturing, such as would occur with such large projects as airplanes or large boats.

16. C: The correct answer is "c." Methods of increasing capacity have an up side and a down side. Overtime pay is higher than regular wages, and companies can afford only a certain amount of it before going outside the budget established for a manufacturing venture. The addition of unaccounted for overtime can upset the entire profit picture of a planned manufacturing operation. But in many cases, it may be the least expensive and most efficient choice among other options—subcontracting, alternate routing, new hiring, upgrading equipment.

17. B: The correct answer is "b." Additional worker training is always a good idea but it is not something that will resolve immediate problems with capacity. When the capacity available is insufficient to produce the capacity required, managers resort to overtime, subcontracting, alternate routing, or the hiring of additional personnel. Each of these methods has disadvantages, although they are all effective at increasing capacity. New and upgraded equipment is often a way to solve capacity bottlenecks, but this is also a longer term solution which should have been addressed during the initial planning stages.

18. A: Answer option "a" is correct because alternate routing refers to an internal remedy for backlogged work. The overload at bottlenecked work centers can be shifted to other underutilized work centers so long as workers are broadly trained to perform several functions. Along with the use of kanban techniques, Japanese manufacturers refined the training of workers so that they could be shifted from the performance of once task to another. This workplace flexibility helped to prevent bottlenecking as backlogged work could be alternatively routed. Alternative routing does not work, however, if all work centers are backlogged or if workers are capable of performing only a single task.

19. A: Answer "a" is the right pick as subcontracting is not an element of production activity control. Production activity control refers to the management and control of a wide array of simultaneous activities on the manufacturing floor. PAC consists of work scheduling; loading of work; tracking systems for work in progress; recordation of all work data; and communications dispatch systems which disseminate data to key points in the manufacturing chain. These production metrics are among the components that must be carefully assessed to ensure profitable manufacture.

20. D: During periods of insufficient capacity, management may exercise the option of adding an additional shift or adding new personnel to an overburdened work center. The additional personnel may be new hires, or they may already be employed by the organization. Either way, the addition of personnel can create unique challenges: union rules and restrictions; budget limitations, and equipment limitations. Financial departments are impacted by new hires and must revised budgets. The addition of new personnel is sometimes restricted by equipment shortages and facility issues.

21. C: The correct answer is "c." When the planners and the master scheduler have agreed that the work is balanced and that there is no threat of bottleneck or overload, they must provide the data to manufacturing supervisors in the form of a daily dispatch list. The dispatch list provides the items that must be completed at the work station and the expected dates of completion. The dispatch list shows when each operation is set to start and finish. The dispatch list also shows pending orders, that is, the work due to arrive from an earlier manufacturing production sequence. The daily dispatch transmits upper level management priorities for inbound work to the shop floor supervisors and floor persons.

22. C: The correct answer is "c." In manufacturing, the method of procurement must be matched to the type of production in a specific facility. Lot-based procurement means that the purchasing agent has obtained price quotes for a particular lot size from a host of potential suppliers. The procurer then makes the decision based on price, quality, and the certainty that delivery can be made on the date the materials are needed. Lot-based procurement means that there is no ongoing commitment to the supplier after the purchase order contract is completed and the materials are delivered to specification.

23. B: The correct answer is "b." Procurement supply scheduling is a manner of materials acquisition that lends itself to continuous flow manufacturing of standard products. The terms of scheduled deliveries are spelled out in a delivery contract. Total volume of material to be delivered under contract may be specified on a yearly basis or the contract may be open ended, that is, requiring the supplier to meet the manufacturer's production schedule. Prices are specified for the length of the contract and cannot be renegotiated until the contract expiration date. The supplier is responsible for balancing the flow of materials to match the manufacturer's demand when this method of scheduling suppliers is used.

24. B: The correct answer is "b." There are three basic procurement systems: lot based procurement; procurement supply scheduling; and the procurement release system which provides the flexibility of meeting long- and short-term manufacturing targets. The procurement release system allows for better planning by a supplier who may have to meet material demands of several different companies.

The procurement release system projects a manufacturing facility's long-term needs and transmits these data to the supplier. The same facility makes a concrete and specific short-term order for supplies with a specific delivery date. The short-term releases are issued on a period basic, either weekly, monthly, quarterly or whatever short-term time frame is necessary for continuous manufacturing.

25. A: Answer "a" is correct but consideration of each machine center as a single unit of productivity is only one aspect of "load profile." A machine center is a group of machines processing a common family of goods that comprises an individual work center and is treated as one unit for planning and routing purposes. A load profile is a report detailing the planned and actual capacity requirements over time. The load profile report, used to calculate efficiency and utilization, is expressed numerically or graphically, not in "subjective terms." Zero inventory is the target level of stock to be maintained in a just-in-time production environment, where inventory is not considered an asset but rather a liability.

26. D: The correct answer is "d." Manufacturers and suppliers sometimes combine efforts in the interest of lean manufacturing. The three chief types of cooperatives supporting this end are strategic alliances, technical-commercial partnering, and operational partnering. In strategic alliances, the manufacturer and the supplier agree to work together to streamline their operations by eliminating duplication of effort. In technical and commercial partnering, the supplier and customer share product development costs. In operational partnering, the supplier agrees to provide standard parts for the manufacturer in a timely, lean, and continuous way.

27. C: The best answer is "c." There are key differences between remanufacturing and repair. In repair, only the worn parts or the parts which have completely failed are replaced. In remanufacturing, nearly all working parts are restored to original, like-new condition. The differences are related to material control functions. In remanufacture, the available materials required are unknown until disassembly. Both remanufacturing and repair operations differ from standard manufacturing, where the availability of raw materials and components is known by consulting the build schedule and all finished products derive from raw materials and/or new components.

28. A: Answer choice "a" best reflects the early objectives of manufacturing design planning. Manufacturing design planning is determined by analysis of the volume-variety characteristics and process type. The volume-variety objectives of manufacturing can be either one of low volume and high variety or one of high volume and low variety. Process types may be broken down into categories like job shop format, batch process format, continuous flow, or mass production processes. These latter concerns for "process type" inform decisions about whether process, product, mixed or cell layouts are to be constructed.

29. C: Choice "c" is correct. The four chief tasks in designing a cell layout are product selection, infrastructure design, work cell layout, and process engineering. It is process engineering, which entails equipment selection, estimates of setup times, assembly times, and labor utilization times. Product selection is a volume-variety concern which impacts cell layout but cells can be configured to accommodate both high- and low-volume product flows. Cell layout (SPU—space planning units) pertains to the physical space that machines and personnel are allotted in the design scheme.

30. A: The best answer choice is "a." Studies show that setup times can account for 30-50% of the time (and cost) in the manufacturing process. Reducing setup times can be accomplished in a variety of ways: standardizing equipment to use common accessories, location, and accessibility of supply materials, uncluttered and well-organized work stations, and worker training. But color coding and standardization of connections is an inexpensive way to reduce setup times and increase manufacturing profits.

31. B: The correct answer is "b." Four general categories of facility layouts are the the cell layout, the project layout approach, the product layout, and the process layout. Cost research data indicate the degree of cost associated with each type of infrastructure layout. The project approach to manufacturing is a type of manufacturing which uses a fixed position to build large "projects" like boats or cargo planes. This type of manufacturing has the highest cost. The second most costly manufacturing layout, according to statistics, is the process layout. The cell layout is more cost efficient than the previous layouts, and is better suited to higher volume, lower variability manufacturing. Least expensive of all is the product layout that is similar to traditional assembly line production with lean-style modifications.

32. D: Option "d" is correct. Synchronous manufacturing refers to the practice of balancing the work in the assembly line so that input is equal to output. A proper balance of workloads must be established as the work product moves through a variety of assembly or finishing stations. The provision of supplier parts should be stable, whether the supply comes from internal or external supply sources. Supply schedules must be consistent with assembly line demand. Line side bin stocks, floor stocks, and backflushing are practical techniques that enhance synchronized manufacturing.

33. D: The correct sequence of operations is the one shown in answer choice "d." The establishment of a production schedule requires cooperation and communication across different operating segments. Scheduling factory production begins with the production plan established at the sales and operations planning meeting. MRP then develops low level manufacturing schedules and organizes the purchase of components that must be ordered. Order scheduling is done by material requirements planners. Detailed scheduling is accomplished at the CRP (capacity requirements level) or at the PAC (production activity control) level.

34. B: Answer choice "b" is the most accurate description of backflushing, a postproduction activity that subtracts supply from the bill of materials rather than from preproduction inventory storage or readiness. Backflushing is particularly useful when the internal supply amounts exceed the amounts of finished products coming off the assembly phases of manufacture. As such, it is more efficient and accurate at keeping system inventory counts in line with actual supply conditions. Backflushing provides a production control mechanism of greater efficiency and less wasted effort that aids synchronous manufacturing.

35. D: Choice "d" is the correct answer. Flow control scheduling is the process of setting production targets and controlling the work centers in such a way that those goals are reached. Flow control scheduling is most often used in assembly-style manufacturing, wherein a product moves along a set path without variation. Efficiency is achieved through mass production and overlapping workloads. Flow control scheduling must be supported by a plant's physical design and layout. Machinery would be positioned in lines rather than having all machines of the same type grouped together.

36. B: The correct answer is "b." Forward loading is defined as the process of loading excess workloads to a forward scheduled period. Inevitably, the scheduled load of materials and products moving downstream toward completion will exceed available capacity. When the forward loading process detects overload, the excess work is shifted into yet another future time period sequence. Overload and ceiling capacity measurement sends signals to the software that responds by adjusting the schedule to move the production forward.

37. B: The correct answer is again "b." Backward loading is a way of treating overloads that shifts the work to an earlier start date. It begins with selecting the order farthest into the future. Work is then moved backward to an earlier fixed start date. It is just the opposite of forward loading, in which excess workloads are put to a forward scheduled period. Both methods acknowledge the ceiling capacity of work centers involved in manufacture, unlike infinite capacity loading which calculates required capacity.

38. C: Answer "c" is the correct one. Forward scheduling with finite loading is a technique for balancing manufacturing load and capacity. Scheduling is based on required start dates and work is loaded in full recogniton of a known and finite manufacturing capacity. The start date is the day that material is released into production. From that day forward, the manufacturing system is loaded to the recognized finite capacity until the order is complete. The end date will vary, dependent on the time it takes to manufacture the required quantity using the available capacity.

39. D: The correct answer is "d." Backward scheduling with finite loading is a technique for balancing manufacturing load and capacity. Scheduling is based on mandatory completion dates which recognize a finite manufacturing capacity. The completion date is the day that the items must be available for higher levels of production. From that day, manufacturing is scheduled backward by loading the manufacturing system to capacity to meet the completion date. This backward loading sets the flexible start date needed in order to meet the completion date.

40. A: Option "a" is the correct answer; process-oriented finite loading looks at the process when it is seeking productivity gains. According to the tenets of this technique, the nature of the process is where improvements can be made, and individual operation delays can be minimized. This streamlining of process carries over to the minimization of order delays. Work is loaded into a process or work center according to the type of process that favorites efficient order fulfillment, although capacity limits are also considered.

41. B: The FALSE answer is "b." The U-shaped cellular flow line is an ideal production process setup for lean operation. A U-shaped cellular flow line is a U-shaped layout of several different kinds of machines that form a one-piece flow line dedicated to specific tasks. The U-shape saves floor space and shortens the travel distance between operators at different machines on the line, facilitates communication and visibility between operators working on products, and can be easily configured to accommodate and produce different products within the same family groups.

42. C: The correct answer is "c." The batch and queue method of old style manufacture is subject to large bottlenecks and frequent stoppages. QRM (quick response manufacturing) is one way of dealing with these problems. QRM is different from other similar forms in that the direction of flow is not always the same. QRM design employs takt time calculation and level scheduling as a basis for designing the individual phases of work within each cell.

43. C: The correct answer is "c." Takt time is a calculation of the maximum production time per unit allowed to produce a product. It is one of the calculations used in QRM (quick response manufacturing), along with level scheduling and flex fences to minimize bottlenecks in the manufacturing process. Level scheduling is a method of evening out the irregularities of demand that can cause production bottlenecks. QRM is an integral part of lean manufacturing that cannot easily be implemented through inventory reduction techniques like kanban.

44. A: Answer option "a" is the correct answer since it is true that QRM flow lines are not configured in the standard linear fashion. The primary focus of QRM is lead time reduction. QRM does not focus on inventory reduction as much as kanban techniques associated with JIT flow line lean production do. There are key differences in the line flow. QRM flow line design is nonlinear, and products can take different paths through the cell. The cells for QRM are designed to accommodate the specific products to be manufactured, rather than with the aim of achieving a smooth, linear flow. QRM methods utilize flexibility to meet varying demand for a wide variety of products.

45. C: The correct answer is "c." The primary focus of QRM is lead time reduction. While efficient administration of QRM processes lowers inventory, QRM does not focus so much on inventory reduction as do the kanban techniques associated with JIT production. QRM lead time reduction processes also result in elimination of waste, which is a natural consequence of the process. QRM consistently measures lead times. In QRM, shrinking lead times results in on-time delivery. The key difference is on matters of focus or emphasis to achieve results. JIT production strives to eliminate waste as a means of continuously improving the process and emphasizes primary performance characteristics such as on time delivery.

46. B: Choice "b" is the correct answer. The choice of a suitable manufacturing process structure will depend on the customer segment to be served. QRM is the better choice when the customer needs custom-engineered items designed with a wide variety of options. JIT lean manufacturing with linear flow lines employing kanban pull systems are suitable for baseline products, which do not have significant product variation. QRM is ideal for companies seeking new market niches, which often have unpredictable and widely varying demand.

47. A: The best answer is "a." POLCA is a hybridized material control system.

It combines many of the features of the card-based kanban technique with materials requirements planning. POLCA was developed to be combined with quick response manufacturing. POLCA works best in businesses that make customized products with a variety of specifications and the system design emphasizes flexibility in work flow and cel structure. POLCA is a card-based system for controlling production that apportions a limited amount of work to cells.

48. D: Answer choice "d" is correct, since all statements describe the characteristics of modern cell configuration. Cellular manufacturing structures may vary significantly, however. There are work cells in which work flows in a single direction, and there are others where the work flows along a variably circuitous path. Characteristics that are common to all types of cellular manufacturing are machines of different types, a cross-trained and highly skilled labor force, and horizontal control of operations that stresses cooperation rather than rank or hierarchy.

49. C: The correct answer, "c," obtained by adding the three categories. The CCC, or cash conversion cycle, is the time it takes for a company to receive an order, manufacture it, deliver the product, and receive cash payment. A short cash conversion cycle indicates that there is efficient use of the plant, equipment, and inventory. A short cash conversion cycle means leaner inventories, and ensures reliability on the supplier side. CCC is a measure of how effectively a company's plant and equipment are utilized.

How to Overcome Test Anxiety

Just the thought of taking a test is enough to make most people a little nervous. A test is an important event that can have a long-term impact on your future, so it's important to take it seriously and it's natural to feel anxious about performing well. But just because anxiety is normal, that doesn't mean that it's helpful in test taking, or that you should simply accept it as part of your life. Anxiety can have a variety of effects. These effects can be mild, like making you feel slightly nervous, or severe, like blocking your ability to focus or remember even a simple detail.

If you experience test anxiety—whether severe or mild—it's important to know how to beat it. To discover this, first you need to understand what causes test anxiety.

Causes of Test Anxiety

While we often think of anxiety as an uncontrollable emotional state, it can actually be caused by simple, practical things. One of the most common causes of test anxiety is that a person does not feel adequately prepared for their test. This feeling can be the result of many different issues such as poor study habits or lack of organization, but the most common culprit is time management. Starting to study too late, failing to organize your study time to cover all of the material, or being distracted while you study will mean that you're not well prepared for the test. This may lead to cramming the night before, which will cause you to be physically and mentally exhausted for the test. Poor time management also contributes to feelings of stress, fear, and hopelessness as you realize you are not well prepared but don't know what to do about it.

Other times, test anxiety is not related to your preparation for the test but comes from unresolved fear. This may be a past failure on a test, or poor performance on tests in general. It may come from comparing yourself to others who seem to be performing better or from the stress of living up to expectations. Anxiety may be driven by fears of the future—how failure on this test would affect your educational and career goals. These fears are often completely irrational, but they can still negatively impact your test performance.

Elements of Test Anxiety

As mentioned earlier, test anxiety is considered to be an emotional state, but it has physical and mental components as well. Sometimes you may not even realize that you are suffering from test anxiety until you notice the physical symptoms. These can include trembling hands, rapid heartbeat, sweating, nausea, and tense muscles. Extreme anxiety may lead to fainting or vomiting. Obviously, any of these symptoms can have a negative impact on testing. It is important to recognize them as soon as they begin to occur so that you can address the problem before it damages your performance.

The mental components of test anxiety include trouble focusing and inability to remember learned information. During a test, your mind is on high alert, which can help you recall information and stay focused for an extended period of time. However, anxiety interferes with your mind's natural processes, causing you to blank out, even on the questions you know well. The strain of testing during anxiety makes it difficult to stay focused, especially on a test that may take several hours. Extreme anxiety can take a huge mental toll, making it difficult not only to recall test information but even to understand the test questions or pull your thoughts together.

Effects of Test Anxiety

Test anxiety is like a disease—if left untreated, it will get progressively worse. Anxiety leads to poor performance, and this reinforces the feelings of fear and failure, which in turn lead to poor performances on subsequent tests. It can grow from a mild nervousness to a crippling condition. If allowed to progress, test anxiety can have a big impact on your schooling, and consequently on your future.

Test anxiety can spread to other parts of your life. Anxiety on tests can become anxiety in any stressful situation, and blanking on a test can turn into panicking in a job situation. But fortunately, you don't have to let anxiety rule your testing and determine your grades. There are a number of relatively simple steps you can take to move past anxiety and function normally on a test and in the rest of life.

Physical Steps for Beating Test Anxiety

While test anxiety is a serious problem, the good news is that it can be overcome. It doesn't have to control your ability to think and remember information. While it may take time, you can begin taking steps today to beat anxiety.

Just as your first hint that you may be struggling with anxiety comes from the physical symptoms, the first step to treating it is also physical. Rest is crucial for having a clear, strong mind. If you are tired, it is much easier to give in to anxiety. But if you establish good sleep habits, your body and mind will be ready to perform optimally, without the strain of exhaustion. Additionally, sleeping well helps you to retain information better, so you're more likely to recall the answers when you see the test questions.

Getting good sleep means more than going to bed on time. It's important to allow your brain time to relax. Take study breaks from time to time so it doesn't get overworked, and don't study right before bed. Take time to rest your mind before trying to rest your body, or you may find it difficult to fall asleep.

Along with sleep, other aspects of physical health are important in preparing for a test. Good nutrition is vital for good brain function. Sugary foods and drinks may give a burst of energy but this burst is followed by a crash, both physically and emotionally. Instead, fuel your body with protein and vitamin-rich foods.

Also, drink plenty of water. Dehydration can lead to headaches and exhaustion, especially if your brain is already under stress from the rigors of the test. Particularly if your test is a long one, drink water during the breaks. And if possible, take an energy-boosting snack to eat between sections.

Along with sleep and diet, a third important part of physical health is exercise. Maintaining a steady workout schedule is helpful, but even taking 5-minute study breaks to walk can help get your blood pumping faster and clear your head. Exercise also releases endorphins, which contribute to a positive feeling and can help combat test anxiety.

When you nurture your physical health, you are also contributing to your mental health. If your body is healthy, your mind is much more likely to be healthy as well. So take time to rest, nourish your body with healthy food and water, and get moving as much as possible. Taking these physical steps will make you stronger and more able to take the mental steps necessary to overcome test anxiety.

Mental Steps for Beating Test Anxiety

Working on the mental side of test anxiety can be more challenging, but as with the physical side, there are clear steps you can take to overcome it. As mentioned earlier, test anxiety often stems from lack of preparation, so the obvious solution is to prepare for the test. Effective studying may be the most important weapon you have for beating test anxiety, but you can and should employ several other mental tools to combat fear.

First, boost your confidence by reminding yourself of past success—tests or projects that you aced. If you're putting as much effort into preparing for this test as you did for those, there's no reason you should expect to fail here. Work hard to prepare; then trust your preparation.

Second, surround yourself with encouraging people. It can be helpful to find a study group, but be sure that the people you're around will encourage a positive attitude. If you spend time with others who are anxious or cynical, this will only contribute to your own anxiety. Look for others who are motivated to study hard from a desire to succeed, not from a fear of failure.

Third, reward yourself. A test is physically and mentally tiring, even without anxiety, and it can be helpful to have something to look forward to. Plan an activity following the test, regardless of the outcome, such as going to a movie or getting ice cream.

When you are taking the test, if you find yourself beginning to feel anxious, remind yourself that you know the material. Visualize successfully completing the test. Then take a few deep, relaxing breaths and return to it. Work through the questions carefully but with confidence, knowing that you are capable of succeeding.

Developing a healthy mental approach to test taking will also aid in other areas of life. Test anxiety affects more than just the actual test—it can be damaging to your mental health and even contribute to depression. It's important to beat test anxiety before it becomes a problem for more than testing.

Study Strategy

Being prepared for the test is necessary to combat anxiety, but what does being prepared look like? You may study for hours on end and still not feel prepared. What you need is a strategy for test prep. The next few pages outline our recommended steps to help you plan out and conquer the challenge of preparation.

Step 1: Scope Out the Test

Learn everything you can about the format (multiple choice, essay, etc.) and what will be on the test. Gather any study materials, course outlines, or sample exams that may be available. Not only will this help you to prepare, but knowing what to expect can help to alleviate test anxiety.

Step 2: Map Out the Material

Look through the textbook or study guide and make note of how many chapters or sections it has. Then divide these over the time you have. For example, if a book has 15 chapters and you have five days to study, you need to cover three chapters each day. Even better, if you have the time, leave an extra day at the end for overall review after you have gone through the material in depth.

If time is limited, you may need to prioritize the material. Look through it and make note of which sections you think you already have a good grasp on, and which need review. While you are studying, skim quickly through the familiar sections and take more time on the challenging parts.

Write out your plan so you don't get lost as you go. Having a written plan also helps you feel more in control of the study, so anxiety is less likely to arise from feeling overwhelmed at the amount to cover.

Step 3: Gather Your Tools

Decide what study method works best for you. Do you prefer to highlight in the book as you study and then go back over the highlighted portions? Or do you type out notes of the important information? Or is it helpful to make flashcards that you can carry with you? Assemble the pens, index cards, highlighters, post-it notes, and any other materials you may need so you won't be distracted by getting up to find things while you study.

If you're having a hard time retaining the information or organizing your notes, experiment with different methods. For example, try color-coding by subject with colored pens, highlighters, or post-it notes. If you learn better by hearing, try recording yourself reading your notes so you can listen while in the car, working out, or simply sitting at your desk. Ask a friend to quiz you from your flashcards, or try teaching someone the material to solidify it in your mind.

Step 4: Create Your Environment

It's important to avoid distractions while you study. This includes both the obvious distractions like visitors and the subtle distractions like an uncomfortable chair (or a too-comfortable couch that makes you want to fall asleep). Set up the best study environment possible: good lighting and a comfortable work area. If background music helps you focus, you may want to turn it on, but otherwise keep the room quiet. If you are using a computer to take notes, be sure you don't have any other windows open, especially applications like social media, games, or anything else that could distract you. Silence your phone and turn off notifications. Be sure to keep water close by so you stay hydrated while you study (but avoid unhealthy drinks and snacks).

Also, take into account the best time of day to study. Are you freshest first thing in the morning? Try to set aside some time then to work through the material. Is your mind clearer in the afternoon or evening? Schedule your study session then. Another method is to study at the same time of day that you will take the test, so that your brain gets used to working on the material at that time and will be ready to focus at test time.

Step 5: Study!

Once you have done all the study preparation, it's time to settle into the actual studying. Sit down, take a few moments to settle your mind so you can focus, and begin to follow your study plan. Don't give in to distractions or let yourself procrastinate. This is your time to prepare so you'll be ready to fearlessly approach the test. Make the most of the time and stay focused.

Of course, you don't want to burn out. If you study too long you may find that you're not retaining the information very well. Take regular study breaks. For example, taking five minutes out of every hour to walk briskly, breathing deeply and swinging your arms, can help your mind stay fresh.

As you get to the end of each chapter or section, it's a good idea to do a quick review. Remind yourself of what you learned and work on any difficult parts. When you feel that you've mastered the material, move on to the next part. At the end of your study session, briefly skim through your notes again.

But while review is helpful, cramming last minute is NOT. If at all possible, work ahead so that you won't need to fit all your study into the last day. Cramming overloads your brain with more information than it can process and retain, and your tired mind may struggle to recall even previously learned information when it is overwhelmed with last-minute study. Also, the urgent nature of cramming and the stress placed on your brain contribute to anxiety. You'll be more likely to go to the test feeling unprepared and having trouble thinking clearly.

So don't cram, and don't stay up late before the test, even just to review your notes at a leisurely pace. Your brain needs rest more than it needs to go over the information again. In fact, plan to finish your studies by noon or early afternoon the day before the test. Give your brain the rest of the day to relax or focus on other things, and get a good night's sleep. Then you will be fresh for the test and better able to recall what you've studied.

Step 6: Take a Practice Test

Many courses offer sample tests, either online or in the study materials. This is an excellent resource to check whether you have mastered the material, as well as to prepare for the test format and environment.

Check the test format ahead of time: the number of questions, the type (multiple choice, free response, etc.), and the time limit. Then create a plan for working through them. For example, if you have 30 minutes to take a 60-question test, your limit is 30 seconds per question. Spend less time on the questions you know well so that you can take more time on the difficult ones.

If you have time to take several practice tests, take the first one open book, with no time limit. Work through the questions at your own pace and make sure you fully understand them. Gradually work up to taking a test under test conditions: sit at a desk with all study materials put away and set a timer. Pace yourself to make sure you finish the test with time to spare and go back to check your answers if you have time.

After each test, check your answers. On the questions you missed, be sure you understand why you missed them. Did you misread the question (tests can use tricky wording)? Did you forget the information? Or was it something you hadn't learned? Go back and study any shaky areas that the practice tests reveal.

Taking these tests not only helps with your grade, but also aids in combating test anxiety. If you're already used to the test conditions, you're less likely to worry about it, and working through tests until you're scoring well gives you a confidence boost. Go through the practice tests until you feel comfortable, and then you can go into the test knowing that you're ready for it.

Test Tips

On test day, you should be confident, knowing that you've prepared well and are ready to answer the questions. But aside from preparation, there are several test day strategies you can employ to maximize your performance.

First, as stated before, get a good night's sleep the night before the test (and for several nights before that, if possible). Go into the test with a fresh, alert mind rather than staying up late to study.

Try not to change too much about your normal routine on the day of the test. It's important to eat a nutritious breakfast, but if you normally don't eat breakfast at all, consider eating just a protein bar. If you're a coffee drinker, go ahead and have your normal coffee. Just make sure you time it so that the caffeine doesn't wear off right in the middle of your test. Avoid sugary beverages, and drink enough water to stay hydrated but not so much that you need a restroom break 10 minutes into the test. If your test isn't first thing in the morning, consider going for a walk or doing a light workout before the test to get your blood flowing.

Allow yourself enough time to get ready, and leave for the test with plenty of time to spare so you won't have the anxiety of scrambling to arrive in time. Another reason to be early is to select a good seat. It's helpful to sit away from doors and windows, which can be distracting. Find a good seat, get out your supplies, and settle your mind before the test begins.

When the test begins, start by going over the instructions carefully, even if you already know what to expect. Make sure you avoid any careless mistakes by following the directions.

Then begin working through the questions, pacing yourself as you've practiced. If you're not sure on an answer, don't spend too much time on it, and don't let it shake your confidence. Either skip it and come back later, or eliminate as many wrong answers as possible and guess among the remaining ones. Don't dwell on these questions as you continue—put them out of your mind and focus on what lies ahead.

Be sure to read all of the answer choices, even if you're sure the first one is the right answer. Sometimes you'll find a better one if you keep reading. But don't second-guess yourself if you do immediately know the answer. Your gut instinct is usually right. Don't let test anxiety rob you of the information you know.

If you have time at the end of the test (and if the test format allows), go back and review your answers. Be cautious about changing any, since your first instinct tends to be correct, but make sure you didn't misread any of the questions or accidentally mark the wrong answer choice. Look over any you skipped and make an educated guess.

At the end, leave the test feeling confident. You've done your best, so don't waste time worrying about your performance or wishing you could change anything. Instead, celebrate the successful completion of this test. And finally, use this test to learn how to deal with anxiety even better next time.

Review Video: Test Anxiety
Visit mometrix.com/academy and enter code: 100340

Important Qualification

Not all anxiety is created equal. If your test anxiety is causing major issues in your life beyond the classroom or testing center, or if you are experiencing troubling physical symptoms related to your anxiety, it may be a sign of a serious physiological or psychological condition. If this sounds like your situation, we strongly encourage you to seek professional help.

Online Resources

Due to our efforts to try to keep this book to a manageable length, we've created a link that will give you access to all of your online resources:

mometrix.com/resources719/cpimeco

It's Your Moment, Let's Celebrate It!

Share your story @mometrixtestpreparation